William Temple's *Analysis* of Sir Philip Sidney's *Apology for Poetry*

medieval & renaissance texts & studies

texts & studies

VOLUME 32

William Temple's *Analysis* of Sir Philip Sidney's *Apology for Poetry*

An Edition and Translation

John Webster

medieval & Renaissance texts & studies
Center for Medieval & Early Renaissance Studies
Binghamton, New York
1984

The Graduate School of The University of Washington
has generously provided a grant
to assist with publication costs

Library of Congress Cataloging in Publication Data

Temple, William, Sir, 1628–1699.
    William Temple's Analysis of Sir Philip Sidney's Apology for poetry.

    (Medieval & Renaissance texts & studies; v. 32)
    English and Latin.
    Includes bibliographical references.
    1. Sidney, Philip, Sir, 1554–1586.   Apologie for poetrie.   2. Poetry
— Early works to 1800.   I. Webster, John, 1944-   .   II. Title.
III. Title: Analysis of Sir Philip Sidney's Apology for poetry.   IV. Series.

PN1031.S653T4513   1984   808.1   83–22060
ISBN 0-86698-066-0

Contents

Acknowledgments

Many people have helped with this work. At the University of Washington I owe special thanks to Alan Fisher and William Streitberger in the English Department, and to Mark Northrup and Linda Rutland in Classics. I want also to thank Father Walter J. Ong, S.J., for reading my translation and for making valuable suggestions as to improvements, and both Charles Schmitt and S. K. Heninger for reading and commenting on the introductory pages. This work would have been much more difficult without the support from the University of Washington Graduate School Research Fund, for a summer study grant and for help with publication costs. Finally, I wish to thank Lord De L'Isle for his generous permission to publish Temple's text, and William A. Elwood for providing me with his transcription of the *Analysis* in order that I could double-check, and improve, my own. Whatever faults remain, this edition is vastly better for the suggestions that these and other scholars have made.

Introduction

William Temple's *Analysis tractationis de Poesi contextae a nobilissimo viro Philippe Sidneio equite aurato* is the earliest known commentary on Sir Philip Sidney's *Apology for Poetry*. [1] Written even before the *Apology* was first published in 1595, Temple's 66–page Latin work treats the entirety of Sidney's text, sometimes objecting, sometimes paraphrasing, at all times trying to describe accurately the course of Sidney's argument. Temple was Sidney's private secretary and he wrote his *Analysis* sometime between the two men's first meeting in 1584 and Sidney's death in 1586. Throughout, Temple addresses Sidney directly, and the text seems to have been intended for Sidney's interest alone. Given the literary importance of the *Apology*, the close relation between Sidney and Temple, and the scope of Temple's remarks on Sidney's argument, Temple's text makes an obvious claim on the attention of Sidney's modern readers. Beyond its particular concern with the *Apology*, however, Temple's text also has the virtue of being an outstanding example of Tudor practical criticism. We know from works like Gabriel Harvey's *Ciceronianus* that Tudor university training was intended to teach students to read texts closely and well, [2] but though the English Renaissance is rich in theoretical statements about what educated readers were to expect from literature, it is poor in examples that show what such readers actually did with the texts they read. No doubt the written form of such analyses seemed quite ordinary to those who wrote them; perhaps for this reason very few works that actually show a reader explicating a literary text ever saw print. [3] Temple's *Analysis*, however, dealing closely and at length with a major Tudor essay, demonstrates clearly what the strengths and weaknesses of such readings could be.

In the body of his text Temple has three aims. The first of these is to explicate the conceptual structure of the *Apology*. Working within a system of logic into which two centuries of "reform" had increasingly brought the subject matter of what had once been called "rhetoric," Temple's structural description explains both what we would call

Sidney's "logic" — the syllogistic forms of his arguments — and Sidney's use of invention to develop and diversify his exposition — a process modern readers will tend to associate with "rhetoric." One very great indirect value of the text, then, is to show in detail the way Tudor rhetorical and logical theory actually was used. Throughout the *Analysis*, we see at first hand how similes were parsed, what purposes various parts of a discourse were understood to serve, and how rhetorical terms with special aesthetic implications were used. Recent scholarship's careful chapters on these matters notwithstanding, it is instructive to see how sixteenth-century usage of terms like "ornamentation," "amplification," or "exaggeration" differs from modern usage.[4] Further, because these sections of the *Analysis* provide a thorough explanatory paraphrase of Sidney's argument, Temple's explication also supplies a record of exactly how he understood the *Apology* in virtually every paragraph. Since our own age is not entirely agreed on what Sidney means in given passages, Temple's paraphrases thus give evidence of a particularly useful kind.[5]

Beyond setting out and explaining the *Apology's* argumentative structure, Temple's second aim in the *Analysis* is to outline and comment upon the organization of Sidney's text. This has been a concern for Sidney scholars at least since Kenneth O. Myrick proposed his theory of the *Apology* as a seven-part judicial oration.[6] What is particularly intriguing about Temple's discussion, however, is that he stresses the *Apology's* expositional features, and not its oratorical features. Temple's understanding of expositional structure is based on what the Renaissance called "Method," a heading under which were grouped several different sixteenth-century attempts to establish a theory of discourse free from the demands of oratorical persuasion.[7] As Temple reads the *Apology*, Sidney's purpose is as much in defining and explaining poetry as it is in defending it. He refers to Sidney's text by the title *On Poetry (de Poesi)*,[8] and his most frequent description of the work, as a *tractatio*, also reflects his understanding of the piece primarily as an explanatory "treatise," or "tract." The final section of his *Analysis* Temple devotes to method, characterizing the *Apology* as having two main parts, a confirmation and a refutation, along with a short "preface" and "epilogue." He then evaluates how well the internal configuration of the confirmation satisfies the requirements of disposition by Method, and suggests ways Sidney's organization might be improved.

The last of Temple's purposes in the *Analysis* is to provide a commentary on the issues of the *Apology*, and in this more critical role Temple inserts paragraphs into his text stating his agreements and disagreements with Sidney's theoretical positions. In general, Temple praises much of what Sidney says, but he also objects to several of Sidney's claims. Where Sidney, for example, argues for poetry's superiority to all other arts, and especially to history and moral philosophy, Temple insists that poetry is to be valued for what it shares with those other arts. Temple will grant that poetry imitates, and that it both teaches and delights, but he will not concede that in these respects poetry is essentially different from other disciplines. Where Sidney emphasizes poetry's rhetorical power to move, Temple emphasizes its dialectical power to represent truth.

These, then, are some of the interests of Temple's text. In order to make them as available as possible to modern readers, the following introduction consists of three parts. In the first, because Temple's work is a "logical" analysis, and because the meaning of the term "logic" has changed greatly over the last four centuries, I explain how Temple's logic worked and how such a system could come to concern itself with a text like Sidney's *Apology*. The second section considers Temple's criticisms of Sidney's aesthetic positions, with the aim both of pointing out specific issues over which the two men disagree, and of suggesting the kind of alternative premises that are implicit throughout Temple's argument. The third part then provides notes on Temple's life, on the text, and on the translation, and it supplies a glossary of Temple's logical terminology. Ordinarily, glossaries follow their texts, but so many of Temple's terms have meanings at odds with modern usage that readers may wish to familiarize themselves with his terms before they actually begin reading the *Analysis* itself.

I

Logic in Tudor England

Temple's *Analysis* of the *Apology* is what Renaissance scholars called a "logical" analysis, but "logic" (or "dialectic" — the words were used interchangeably in Tudor England) did not mean the same thing to Temple that it means to us.[9] Few of us think of logic as a necessary part of a general education; instead we associate logic with a specialized and abstract precision of language, a concern with science and mathematics, a perfect cold reason. But in Temple's understanding logic's main functions were to clarify the kinds of statements that could be made about the world, and to explain the proper ways such statements could be combined to create meaningful discourse. The syllogism has a role in this, but it is a concern subordinate to the art's more general aims. Time and again, humanist logicians point out that logic's task is not just to argue or prove, but to explain and to teach. Thus, for Rudolph Agricola, logic is the art of "setting out probably whatever thing is proposed"; for Philip Melanchthon it is the "art or way of teaching rightly, in proper order, and perspicuously"; for Peter Ramus it is "the art of discoursing well." Even more directly, "He that speaketh logique," Thomas Wilson tells us, "speaketh nothing els but reason."[10]

The humanist logics of Tudor England, then, should not be thought of as abstruse and specialized texts. Rather, their aim is to provide an organized study of thought and communication, a systematic aid to the sophisticated use of language. All men use logic, Tudor scholars would have said, whether they are logicians or not; the "logician" differs from the rest of us only in having studied the best thinking of the best writers, and in having abstracted from them the general rules for perfected discourse. As Abraham Fraunce writes in his *Lawiers Logike*, "Artificiall logike is gathered out of diuers examples of naturall reason, which is not any Art of Logike, but that engrauen gift and facultie of wit and reason shining in the discourses of seuerall men. . . ."[11] Indeed, so central is logic to knowing, that it is mankind's best response to the limits on understanding placed on us by the Fall. Wilson explains:

> Manne, by nature hath a sparke of knowlege, and by the secrete woorking of God, iudgeth after a sorte, and discerneth good from euil. Before the fal of Adam, this knowelege was perfeicte, but through offence, darkenesse folowed, and the bright light was taken awaie. Wisemen therefore, consideryng the weakenesse of mannes witte, and the blindnesse also, wherin we are all drouned: inuented this Arte, to helpe us the rather, by a natural order, to find out the trueth. For though before Adams falle, knowlege was natural, and came without labour, yet no one manne can now of him selfe, atteine the trueth in all thinges, without helpe and diligent learnyng (pp. 9–10).

Wilson called his logic *The Rule of Reason,* and his paragraph here makes clear how general he took the scope of the logical enterprise to be. For him, we are helpless without logic, for "neither can we dooe any thing, without the helpe of reason, to guide al our actions" (p. 8).

In late Tudor England there were principally two systems of logic in use, and there was a spirited debate over their respective merits. Modern scholarship has tended to emphasize the differences between these two schools, but in fact the two agree in their general aims and interests far more often than they disagree, and both ultimately derive from the same source, Agricola's *De Inventione*.[12] The first and more traditional of the two logics was Philip Melanchthon's; the second was an expressly reformist version by the Frenchman Peter Ramus. Temple took Ramus as his model; by virtue of a pamphlet war with the Oxford logician Everard Digby over the value of Ramus' Method, and by publishing in 1584 a long, explanatory edition of Ramus' *Dialectica,* Temple became England's best known Ramist.[13] Because the emphases and vocabulary of Temple's *Analysis* reflect this Ramist perspective, I shall be outlining the Ramist system in the pages that follow, but I want also to emphasize that while Ramist logic is organized and developed differently from Melanchthon's, both logicians share the humanist tendency towards pragmatic, "reasonable" logic, both see logic's primary usefulness to lie in teaching and moral reasoning, and both transfer much of what traditionally had been concerns of rhetoric into their more broadly defined logics. Their two systems were by no means antithetical; students could and obviously did move from one system to the other. Though much declamation (especially against Ramism) is to be found late in the century, a Ramist like Gabriel Harvey could still praise Thomas Wilson's Melanchthon-based texts for their "great variety of rhetorique, logique, and much other learning," even complimenting Wilson's rhetoric by placing it in the same elite class with the *Instituta Oratoria*.[14] Though different, the two traditions are still cut from the same cloth.

Ramism

Nowhere is logic any more a practical art of reason than in the Ramist system. Agricola had defined logic as an art of explanation, or teaching, whose end was to present an idea as fully and persuasively as its nature would allow; Ramus keeps this expository bias, defining logic as an art of discoursing well (*ars bene disserendi*). In itself, concern with the composition and analysis of texts is not unusual among sixteenth-century logics, but Ramus focuses his logic so intently on the arts of composition that its language and assumptions virtually prevent it from doing anything else. Defined by the tasks of explication and, especially, of organization, Ramus' logic makes syllogistic demonstration — which is the heart of what twentieth-century readers generally understand logic to be—a distinctly secondary concern. Only when clarity of statement will not by itself suffice to make something clear and credible will one be forced to use syllogisms in order to "prove" in the modern sense of establishing certainty through deductive reasoning.

As a system designed to give precepts for clear explanation, then, and conversely, for the analysis of any given discourse in order to lay bare its logical and expository structure, Ramist logics are organized into two books, the first of which treats Invention, the second, Judgment. The book of Invention is straightforward and uncomplicated. Except for the first chapters in which a number of basic terms are defined, it is entirely devoted to explaining one by one each of Ramus' "topics," or "places of invention." These are arranged hierarchically, and as such they lend themselves to a kind of tree diagram, or table. With the topics laid out in this way, not only can one see them all at a glance, one can also see the relations that hold between them, and thus this scheme stands as a kind of summary of the whole book (see figure 1, p. 17).

The general functions of the topics are the same in Ramist logics as in other humanist logics; they act as key headings, or places, such as "definition," "genus," "species," "cause," "effect," each of which names a particular kind of relation that can obtain between the subject and predicate of a statement. In Agricola's *De Inventione,* there are twenty-four such places, and taken together they are intended to include all one could possibly say on any given subject. If, for example, we were given the subject "man," by using each of the places listed above we could form the following statements: from the place of definition: "Man is a living creature endued with reason;" from genus: "Man is an animal;" from species: "There is a man named Peter;" from cause: "God created man;" from effect: "Man builds cities." This process of "drawing from" the places could be continued through all twenty-four, and, from many places, more than a single proposition could be taken. The place of comparison, for example, Agricola's twenty-second place, has a limitless capacity for forming arguments, since there is no end to the ways a particular subject will be "like" something else.

Given such a network of conceptual categories, Ramists make use of them in two ways. One can either classify the propositions one encounters when reading a given text—the process called "analysis"—or one can use the set of places as a kind of hunting ground in which to search out terms that either can be used to construct syllogisms, or can serve as material to be organized into longer discourses. In this hunting mode—the process called "genesis"—the object is to make a first step towards a full-fledged explanation or treatise by surveying

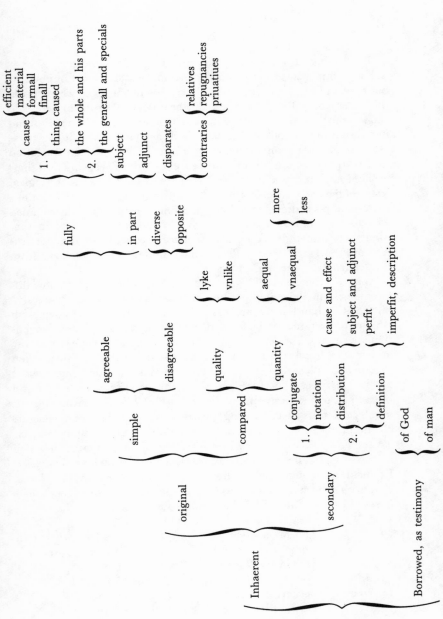

Figure 1. Ramus' Book of Invention From Abraham Fraunce, *The Lawiers Logike*

and collecting all knowledge relevant to a given subject.

For Temple, it is clearly analytic invention that is most important, but how, in fact, does one "analyze" a statement? Suppose we are given the statement, "God created man." The analytical problem here is to classify the two terms of the sentence ("God" and "man") as they stand in relation to each other. Because "God" as man's maker is the cause of man, and man, conversely, is the effect of God, the logical relation they hold to each other is that of "cause" to "effect." Having said that, we have explained the statement's structure by reference to the logical status of the two terms. In Temple's *Analysis*, for example, when Sidney writes that poets drew "with their charming sweetnes the wild vntamed wits to an admiration of knowledge,"[15] Temple will explain that Sidney's argument is taken from the place of effect, since the "admiration of knowledge" is an "effect" which Sidney believes follows from the "charming sweetnes" of poets.

Analysis, then, is useful wherever one's task is to explain how different terms in a given proposition are related to each other. "Genesis," on the other hand, is the process used to find terms of one's own with which propositions can be formed. As in analysis, the places of invention are central, but here they serve as devices by which one can survey and marshall everything one knows about a subject. Since taken together the pieces are supposed to include all the meaningful ways any two terms can be related, by going through them one by one and by asking the questions appropriate to each place — e. g., what are this term's causes? its effects? its opposites? — we ought to be able to generate all the predications which can be made about any possible subject. To see how this works, consider Abraham Fraunce's table in which he shows how different terms, or "arguments," as they are known in Ramist terminology, can be drawn from their corresponding places. Fraunce's subject is "man," and each of the arguments Fraunce elicits is said to be an "affection" that "man" possesses:

	god his maker		effect procreated	
	bodie his matter		effect material	
	reason his forme		effect formale	
Man	godes glorie, his ende	hathe the	effect finale	
referred	actions his effectes	affection	cause	
to	earthe his subject	of the	adjunct	
	riches his adjuncts		subject	
	tree a disparat		disparat	
	beast a contrarie		contarie	
	angel his equal		equale	

Blubb his lyke	lyke
human, the notation	name interpreted
bodie as his part	whole
world whole	part
liuing creature general	special
Paul hys special	general
reasonable, liuinge,	thinge,
creature, his	defined[16]
definition	

As far as Fraunce goes here, his scheme provides seventeen possible predications which can be made about "Man." From effect, for example, we can say that "God made man;" from the adjunct we can say that "Man lives on earth;" or from definition we can say that "Man is a reasonable, living creature." But this table is only a start, since, as I have already suggested, from places like adjunct or comparison we can draw many different arguments. Thus, in theory at least, if we can canvass the places thoroughly we will have "invented" (or better, "found," the earlier meaning of *"invenire"*) all the material we need from which to create a complete discourse.

Once one has mastered the list of places and what they mean, neither "analysis" nor "genesis" will present much difficulty, at least as far as invention is concerned. Genesis does presuppose that one actually possesses a basic supply of commonplace information concerning the causes, effects, adjuncts and so on of one's given subject, but beyond that, the system itself is simple. And analysis is only a matter of parsing by relational categories. Though the ostensible purpose of analysis is to make explicit the basis upon which one will have to judge whether a particular statement is true or false, its effective purpose is the heuristic one of itemizing a discourse's content and focussing on just what is said and how. Clearly, this logic's major analytic virtue is less to be found in philosophical nicety than in providing a systematic means of paying close attention to a text, thereby encouraging precision in reading and in composition.

Where Invention is concerned with either the finding or the classification of individual terms, Ramus' second part of logic, Judgment, is concerned with their combination into actual units of discourse. "As Invention treats the precepts of inventing arguments, so judgment includes the precepts of combining and disposing the arguments that one has invented. Invention invents causes, effects, subjects, adjuncts. . . . Judgment disposes and combines cause with effect, subject with adjunct."[17] Ramus divides Judgment (or "Disposi-

tion"—Ramus uses the terms interchangeably) into three parts: judgment by axiom, judgment by syllogism, and judgment by Method.
Of these, axiomatic and syllogistic judgment provide the basic pro-
positional units of discourse, and methodical judgment (or simply
"Method") provides precepts by which propositions can be organized
into large-scale discourse. Because of Method's exclusively organizational concerns, it is the part of logic that most fully characterizes
Ramus' interest in exposition.

Disposition by axiom, the first part of Judgment, is the arranging
together of two terms, along with a verb of some sort, to produce a
proposition, or what the Ramists called an "axiom." "God" and "man"
are each simple "arguments;" we can make them into an "axiom" by
arranging them with a verb: "God created man." Axiomatic disposition is thus the first step towards complex discourse. Yet to have for-
mulated an axiom is not enough; we must also judge our creation as
to whether it is true or false. For the most part, this judgment is accomplished by simple inspection. As Ramus himself puts it, "if a simple axiom is certain and believable for us, it is judged to be true."[18]
There is in this an obvious faith in intuitive judgment, but if we keep
in mind that it is the general discourse of reason and not the discourse
of scientific certainty with which the humanist logics are concerned,
then Ramus' streamlined version of "axiomatical judgment" (as this
truth-by-inspection judgment is called) makes good practical sense.
In writing a treatise on "temperance," for example, or a commentary
on Vergil's *Aeneid*, it would be cumbersome in the extreme to have
to establish every proposition by deduction from first principles. No
one did it then; no one does it now. As Fraunce remarks, if axioms
"bee not sometimes certayne and so iudged by axiomaticall iudgment,
and graunted; there will be no ende of making syllogismes" (*LL*, p.
98a).

But if the value of most axioms can be decided by inspection, there
are still uncertain axioms, and for these one has recourse to syllogism.
Here the object is to find grounds for either accepting or rejecting a
particular axiom, and that, in Ramistic as much as in any other
humanistic logic, is accomplished by searching the places of invention for an appropriate third term with which to construct a valid
syllogistic deduction. Suppose, by way of example, we were uncertain about the truth of the axiom: "Paris is not a good shepherd." Like
all simple axioms this has two arguments, "Paris," and "good shepherd,"
disposed together. To form a syllogism, however, we need a third argument which can be disposed with each of the given axiom's terms to
give us premises from which"Paris is not a good shepherd" can follow

as a conclusion. What the places do is to supply a list of general headings which can help us in a mental search for the right third term. Not every place will supply what we need, but if we visit them each in turn, we have a good chance of finding something. In the present case Abraham Fraunce finds a useful third term in the place of "adjunct." Thus, because it is an adjunct of good shepherds that they are not idle, and because it was a Renaissance commonplace that Paris *was* idle, "idle"-ness fits our requirements for a third term and we can form the following syllogistic demonstration:

> A good shepherd is not idle,
> But Paris is idle.
> Therefore, Paris is not a good shepherd.   (*LL*, p.105b)

Q. E. D., and what goes for this axiom ought to be possible for all, though again, it should be stressed that because syllogism is to function only as a kind of court of appeal from the more usual axiomatic judgment, the over-all process of Judgment is nothing like a series of deductive moves from *a priori* principles. Rather it is understood as the establishing of ranks of common sense propositions, some of which may need to be "sent to syllogisme," as Fraunce puts it, but only when they are not "playne inough of themselues" (*LL*, p. 98a). Formal inference is thus very much subordinated to the discourse of traditionally received, "certain and believable" opinion. (For descriptions of Ramus' different syllogistic forms, see the Glossary below.)

The third part of Judgment in Ramus' system was "Method," and under this heading Ramist logics give precepts for organizing single axioms into extended discourse. Though not the first logician to discuss such organizational matters, or even to use the term "Method," Ramus attributed so much importance to it that by mid-century Method had become something like the trademark of his school. Ramus himself over-valued Method; to him it was a means to scientific discovery as well as to literary composition. But not all his followers were as naive as he, and for Temple the value of Method was entirely in the help it offered for the discursive presentation of difficult subjects.[19]

That the organization of large-scale discourse should be a concern of logic follows from the humanist claim that logic should be an "art of teaching." The result of this concern is important, for by "teaching" the humanists generally meant any discourse, written or oral, whose object was a clear and inclusive explanation of a given subject. In our own age, the conventions of expository writing (as we would call such "teaching") are largely taken for granted, and we may not appreciate the conceptual difficulty of formulating principles of disposition based solely on a subject's own requirements. We tend to take such properties of expository discourse as "coherence" or "development" as commonplace and well-defined goals. But in the early sixteenth century, organized theories of discourse had little to say on such matters. Instead, it is oratory that dominates discussions of organizational technique, and as valuable and interesting as oratory is, its forms and conventions are also limited by having been designed to address particular issues on particular occasions, and to address them in such a way as to elicit carefully planned responses from one's hearers. But if one's purpose is not to persuade or to move, but simply to explain or make clear, if one has no particular case to plead but wants only to consider a theme generally and in all its parts, then a mode of discourse that depends on the pros and cons of argumentation or on the shaping of one's audience's thoughts and feelings will no longer be appropriate. What is needed is a clearly defined alternative to oratory. This the logicians set out to supply, and again, they base their solution on the places of invention.

As an *ars docendi*, logic becomes responsible for both the content and the form of teaching discourse, and to begin with, at least, both these functions were greatly facilitated by the places. I have already explained how the places can be used collectively to survey one's entire mental holdings, and how by drawing a subject through all the places one ought to end up with an encyclopedic over-view of whatever it was one started with. But because in practice the use of all twenty-four places would be cumbersome, early efforts to make the expositional problems of teaching an explicitly logical matter select just those topics that will pull together what is most relevant and essential to a given subject's presentation. These selected places are grouped under the rubric "Method," which Wilson describes as "the readie waie how to teache and sette foorthe any thing plainely, and in ordre" (p. 43), and to accomplish this task the places are given to us in the form of questions. Thus Melanchthon's *Erotemata Dialectica* (1547) lists the following questions, explaining that these will show the way "through impenetrable and briar-covered places" and will "establish the pertinent matters concerning the subject and set them out in order":

1. What does the term mean?
2. Does the thing exist?
3. What is it?
4. What are its parts?
5. What are its species?

6. What are its causes?
7. What are its effects?
8. What are its characteristics?
9. To what is it related?
10. What can be opposed to it?   (p. 424)

Most important here for the history of exposition, these questions not only define the scope of a discourse, but also define its order. Thus in this scheme one begins a discourse not, as one would an oration, with an effort to soften one's audience, nor does one follow with a five or seven part structure designed first to show one's strongest case, and then to undermine an opponent's possible objections. Those are audience-oriented tactics, and they have no place in straightforward explanation. Instead we begin a teaching discourse with general questions of definition and existence, and we then proceed to increasingly specific information about the subject's parts and adjuncts.

When Ramus comes to the problem of Method, he makes two significant changes. First, for Melanchthon's limited list of ten questions, Ramus substitutes the entire framework of the places of invention, thereby increasing the kinds of information that will fall within Method's scope. Where Melanchthon's Method directed its users to just ten general kinds of inquiry, Ramus' directs them to as many questions as there are places. Second, Ramus makes Method an *a posteriori* process. Instead of prescribing, as Melanchthon did, an order fixed by a pre-determined set of questions, Ramus instructs us that organization can take place only after all invention and all axiomatic disposition is complete, and that we are then to dispose our axioms by beginning with the axiom that is most general, proceeding by descending levels of generality until we reach the level of our least general, most specific axioms. In place of Melanchthon's fixed order, then, Ramus gives us simply a general ordering principle. Thus if we were, for example, to explain the art of logic, Ramus would have us begin not with specific examples of syllogism or of Method (as an inductive order might), but with his general definition of logic as the art of discoursing well. Then, with the art defined (and with the terms of the definition explained), we would follow by dividing logic into its two main parts of Invention and Judgment, and we would explain each in turn. Within the discussion of each part we would again begin with general definitions and explanations, and we would then take up each part's sub-parts. We would, in fact, follow exactly the order that Ramus himself follows in his *Dialectic*, and which I have been following in this summary.

In Temple's redaction of Ramism, this basic ordering principle is retained, but Temple pays more attention than does Ramus to the practical problems of exposition. Because Ramus limits his examples to those general arts like logic or grammar which proceed neatly by definition, division, and so on, his interest in Method often seems defined as much by its formal elegance as by its effective presentation of material. Thus Ramus likes to reflect on the symmetry and order of Method, and in his explanations he speaks of it as the perfect embodiment of a kind of quasi-Platonic ideal: "This Method seems to me a kind of long chain of gold, as Homer imagines, whose links are its degrees, dependent one upon the other, and all linked so precisely together that nothing can be taken out without breaking the order and continuity of the whole thing" (*Dialectique*, p. 146).

But the real difficulties of explanation come when one deals with subjects where such obvious skeletal outlines are not so easily discernible. Temple understands this, and his discussion keeps its focus squarely on the help Method provides for making the obscure clear: "All things," Temple writes, "that come under the keen insight of judgment are either clear and obvious by nature, or dubious and confused. Those which are clear of themselves, and include a certain native transparency, these, by virtue of an illumination summoned from somewhere, require no effort. . . . But truly those things whose nature is a little more obscure and inverted, these accept from other things the light which they do not have in themselves, by whose force obscurity vanishes, and confusion disappears" (*Dialecticae*, pp. 115–16). Temple knows that disposition by Method is an abstract task, and that it is not always easy to decide what is more general or more clear in any one situation. Thus his advice tends towards the open-ended: "Follow this therefore: Whatever contains the causes and subjects of other things; whatever can be understood and explained before other things are explained and understood; whatever inheres in the rest; whatever can be said from which the consequence cannot be derived by conversion; this is what is known more absolutely, what is more general" (p. 136). Though Temple clearly maintains the basic Ramist position, his advice, especially in its second clause, allows much room for maneuver. Temple does not forget that the final purpose of Method is to explain clearly, not to be formally elegant, and when he describes and evaluates Sidney's Method in the *Apology*, it is in terms of these expository values that his remarks are made.

Logic and Rhetoric

Ramistic logic has been termed a "rhetoricized" logic; it should by now be clear why. For Ramus, the entire art of expository composition, from the "finding" and developing of a subject all the way to its final disposition into a large-scale structure, is handled by logic, and further, logic is also charged with the explication of any sort of semantic relation. In its "analytic" mode, logic is responsible for much of what we would now call "rhetorical analysis," or even "literary criticism." Questions about how ideas are developed, why they are set out as they are, what strategies are employed for what ends — these are all issues to which logic is asked to speak. As a result, the body of Temple's *Analysis* is replete with terms that to modern ears have a distinctly rhetorical cast, but which to Temple are the bread and butter of logic. When Sidney develops an idea through comparison or allusion or syllogism, Temple describes his procedure with verbs like *ornare*, or *exornare*. Exemplification is rendered by *amplificare, exaggerare,* or *illustrare,* and at other points Temple's logical vocabulary extends to *laudare, commendare, docere,* and *explicare,* again terms modern readers might sooner think rhetorical than logical. Or consider the parsings of simile. For Temple this is a logical issue, even when the comparison involved is fictional. As Fraunce writes in the *Lawiers Logike*: "Fayned similitudes haue like force with others: and here . . . *Esopicall* fables haue a very good grace. So *Menenius Agrippa* vsing the tale of the rebellion betweene the belly and other partes of the body: and comparing that with the rebellion betweene the common people and senators of Roome, perswaded those that were fled to the holie hill, quicklie to returne home to Roome, and become conformable citizens" (p. 73a). In Fraunce's world, it was logic, not rhetoric, through which Agrippa kept the Roman peace.

With so much of the art of communication given to logic, the art of rhetoric was left in Temple's Ramist system with only the two subjects of Elocution and Delivery.[20] Of these, Elocution is the more important; Delivery, because its task is to describe techniques of voice and gesture, is difficult to describe in words, and in Ramism, as in all humanist rhetorics, the subject is handled with dispatch. Elocution, on the other hand, is treated at length in two sections. The first of these concerns Tropes, or single words that have been "turned" from their ordinary meanings; the second concerns Figures, which involve various schematized groupings of words and even whole speeches.

Examples of Tropes include metaphor, metonyme, synechdoche, irony; examples of Figures include rhyme and meter, patterned repetitions of sound, special conceits of rhetorical situation like apostrophe and personification. Because Temple's *Analysis* spends little time describing Sidney's use of these devices I offer no full description of them here. But it is important to see that what makes all these matters rhetorical and not logical is the idea that Tropes and Figures are "a certayne decking of speach, whereby the vsual and simple fashion thereof is changed to that which is more elegant and conceipted."[21] They lend force and liveliness to a discourse, but unlike such logical techniques as comparison by simile, they are not thought to have the power to explain ideas or to make meanings more clear.

As an independent art, then, rhetoric's role in this system seems a minor one. Still, the actual effect of defining rhetoric so narrowly can easily be exaggerated. No Ramist rhetorician thought his art to be independent of logic; Gabriel Harvey was Cambridge prelector in Rhetoric when he outlined in the *Ciceronianus* the course of study his students were to take, but he makes clear to all that critical reading is a logical as well as a rhetorical concern. In reading Cicero Harvey asks his students to examine the logical elements of Cicero's enthymemes, his Method, his strategies of indirection ("crypses"). He then goes on:

> And since amplitude of content supports [Cicero's] harmony of diction as the soul supports the body, let us also employ the double analysis which we have hitherto been using and apply both rhetoric and dialectic continually in all his writings and with special care in every period. Let us make rhetoric the expositor of the oratorical embellishments and the arts which belong to its school, and dialectic the expositor of invention and arrangement. Both these will be very pleasant for me to teach, and believe me, they will be very useful for you to learn.[22]

In a "double analysis" such as Harvey describes, the jurisdictional lines between logic and rhetoric are virtually superfluous. To be a rhetorician requires that one be a logician; the reverse, judging from Temple's *Analysis*, is no less true. Unfortunately, though Harvey is eloquent in exhorting us to read and to analyze, he himself gives only precept and not example of what he would have us do. Yet precisely because the conventional boundaries of logic and rhetoric have shifted so since the sixteenth century, precepts are meaningless without a sense of how one would actually make use of them. To see clearly how the critical process Harvey so highly prizes actually works, it it thus to texts like Temple's *Analysis* that we must look.

II

Temple on the "Apology"

Beyond its usefulness as a practical example of how a sixteenth-century scholar read closely, Temple's *Analysis* will interest modern readers for its explicit commentary on the *Apology*. Temple is dependent on Sidney, but he is nevertheless willing to disagree strongly with his employer — testimony to Sidney's intellectual generosity as well as to Temple's own critical integrity. To be sure, almost every objection Temple makes is paired with an exaggerated bow to Sidney's eminence, and one amusement in reading Temple comes from learning to recognize these apostrophes to Sidney's brilliance as the almost certain notice that Temple is about to contradict his master. In general, of course, he praises Sidney's essay, but as one pieces together Temple's disparate comments, it is also clear that his basic aesthetic premises are distinctly different from Sidney's. Because everything Temple says, however, is in reaction to positions Sidney takes, I want to begin by outlining those aspects of Sidney's aesthetic with which Temple disagrees most clearly.

With a poet's wit and force, Sidney argues in the *Apology* for a conception of English verse founded on what he conceives to be poetry's special and essential power to move. In living well, Sidney tells us, "moouing is of a higher degree then teaching," and poetry is the art that can move us best. As Sidney says, "Nowe therein of all Sciences ... is our Poet the Monarch. For he dooth not only show the way, but giueth so sweete a prospect into the way, as will intice any man to enter into it" (p. 172). Poetry, then, has an active, moral role in shaping the world that is matched among other disciplines only by the preacher's. For though the poet's imagination "delivers forth" universals of virtuous action, and thus imitates those Ideas that underlie and inform the actualities of the ordinary world, this imitation for Sidney is not the real difficulty. Our greatest problem in a fallen world is that our "will" is often unwilling to do good, even when it knows what good is. "[O]ur erected wit maketh vs know what perfection is," Sidney tells us, "and yet our infected will keepeth vs from reaching vnto it" (p. 157). Consequently, though other arts like history and philosophy can inform us about good and evil, only poetry can "gild" "brazen" nature such that the resulting "speaking picture" will compel us to action. As Murray Krieger has remarked, the final triumph of poetry for Sidney comes with its effect on the human will: "it is for us, in aping the fictional product of his wit, to bring the perfections of an ought-to-be reality into a brazen world of will...."[23] In Sidney's hands, the doctrine of poetic imitation becomes the means by which man can at least in part recover that perfect world long lost by "that first accursed fall of *Adam*" (p. 157).

Sidney's view of poetry, then, is of a unique, almost messianic vehicle by which the true end of life can be attained, but if his theory was certain to please poets and the readers of poets, it also was bound to elicit skepticism from those scholars who practiced any of the arts which suffered in Sidney's artful comparisons. Temple was precisely such a man, Cambridge-trained in philosophy and logic, and his comments on the *Apology* reflect the positions of a moral philosopher responding to a poet. Many of his remarks are thus qualifications aimed simply to deny poetry exclusive rights to the effective achievement of "the end of well dooing," but Temple also wants to argue that as a vehicle of reason and insight, poetry is a logical art. Thus, where Sidney emphasizes poetry's power to move, Temple consistently shifts this focus to issues of truth and understanding.

If Temple's claim that poetry is a "logical" art seems odd to us, it would not have seemed so in Tudor England. I have already explained logic's position as that subject which deals with reasonable thought; it follows from this conception of logic's role among the arts that any discipline which functions by virtue of thought and language will necessarily make use of logic's precepts. As the study of the general processes that underlie human thinking, logic — the *ars artis*, or *scientia scientiarum*, as commonplace had it — was the over-arching discipline under which all modes of knowing were ranked. Nor was this view held only by self-interested logicians. For many traditional theorists the question was not whether poetry was "logical," since no one doubted its dependence on thought and language. Instead there were disputes over just which part of logic best fitted poetry's particular mode of thought.[24] When Temple raises the question of poetry and logic, then, he is not breaking new ground. He is, however, raising questions of knowledge and truth which, from his point of view, Sidney overlooks, and the first place he argues these issues is in response to Sidney's definition of poetry.

"Poesie therefore," Sidney writes, "is an arte of imitation, for so *Aristotle* termeth it in his word *Mimesis*, that is to say, a representing, counterfetting, or figuring foorth: to speak metaphorically, a speaking picture: with this end, to teach and delight" (p. 158). Temple's response to this definition divides the issue of imitation from the issues of teaching and delighting, and when he speaks to the issues of teaching and delighting his aim is simply to counter Sidney's claim for poetry's uniqueness among the arts. Temple's argument turns on the difference between a definition and a description. In strictly logical terms, "defining" characteristics are only those which mark off the specialness of a thing, rather than simply describing it. Thus while a sentence like "Man is an animal" is a true description of man, it is not a proper definition, since lions and rabbits are just as much animals as is man. On the other hand, "Man is a risible, rational animal" *is* a defining statement, since the qualities of risibility and rationality, at least by Renaissance tradition, are peculiar to man alone. In the present case, Temple tells us, "teaching and delighting" cannot be defining ends of poetry since neither is peculiar only to poetry: "The faculty of teaching, since it is made up of arguments disposed by axiom, syllogism and method, will belong not to poetry, but to dialectic" (p. 83). Similarly, though poetry certainly delights, so do many other things, and thus again, it is inappropriate to make delight a defining end of poetry: "Even if delight can proceed from the sweetness of poetry, nevertheless it also flows from other places ... " (p. 83). Though Temple in no way denies poetry's ability to teach or to delight, neither will he let Sidney appropriate these valuable ends to poetry alone.

In contrast to this technical argument over poetry's provenance, Temple's answer to Sidney's definition of poetry as an art of imitation raises a more complicated aesthetic issue. In the paragraphs immediately preceding his definition, Sidney has prepared his way by suggesting that poetry's fictive character allows it alone to escape being subject to nature: "There is no arte deliuered to mankinde that hath not the workes of Nature for his object, without which they could not consist, and on which they so depend, as they become Actors and Players, as it were, of what Nature will have set foorth.... Onely the Poet, disdayning to be tied to any such subiection, dooth growe in effect another nature, in making things either better then Nature bringeth forth, or, quite a newe ..." (p. 156). According to Sidney, then, the power to invent fictions belongs to poetry alone. For Temple, however, the question of how something is invented, whether fictional or not, raises issues which only the art of reason can fully explain. "You want the essential nature of poetry to be understood as a certain kind of fiction-making. But can it be that such a making is anything but the invention of something that has never existed?" (p. 81). How can one imitate meaningful scenarios, Temple would ask, feigned or not, except through the conceptual conventions that any language presupposes and that dialectic codifies as Invention? "Anyone who makes fictions," Temple says, "creates what are logical arguments [i.e., rational concepts]— namely causes, effects, subjects, adjuncts, contraries and comparisons...." When Ovid, for example, creates the realm of the sun, while that realm is obviously a fiction, it was nevertheless created by Ovid's feigning "an efficient cause by which it was constructed, matter out of which it was put together, and adjuncts by which it was decorated." But Ovid's poetic feigning of such things is not essentially different from his inventing them logically, and therefore, "fiction-making will be the same as the [logical] invention of something that does not exist." A thought may be a fiction, but it will only have sense in the first place by virtue of conventions of language and categories of thought, and it is precisely these which form the subject matter of dialectic. Consequently, when poets make fictions, "they do so not by some gift peculiar to poetry, but by the faculty of the art of dialectic" (p. 83).

What is immediately clear here is that Temple's remarks reflect a notion of what is involved in defining poetry that is very different from Sidney's. This is most easily seen in the way Temple substitutes the word *fictio*, a "making," or a "fiction," for Sidney's word "imitation." The shift in meaning is not great; Sidney's "art of imitation" is in fact "an art of making," and Temple does not falsify Sidney to make the change. Yet the shift reveals Temple's very different approach. For there is a way in which "imitation" gets one around the very issue Temple cares most about. If the poet's task is defined simply as an "imitation," or "representation," then there may be presupposed by the logic of these terms that something already exists "out there" — either in nature or in the poet's mind's eye — from which the poet can work. To define poetry as a "speaking picture" implies the existence of objects it can be a picture of, and if that implication is allowed, one can easily underestimate or even overlook the questions of how one conceives of these objects in the first place, of how one knows that one's representing of them is in fact "true." Temple's word *fictio*, on the other hand, has no such implication; indeed it suggests something like the reverse. To describe poetry as an art of making leads immediately to the question of how the poet's images arise, of how he knows what to write about to begin with, and Temple's interest in these questions explains why his discussion focuses entirely on the question of invention. Fictions must come from somewhere; where they come from and how they arise seem to Temple the affair of logic.

Implicit throughout this discussion, then, is Temple's feeling that Sidney's definition takes for granted the whole process by which the poet first conceptualizes and then embodies the "Idea" he sets out to imitate. Though Sidney tells us that the poet can conceive of universals, and that they are in fact what keep his fictions from being "wholly imaginative," "like castles in air," still, should anyone ask how we are to be sure that the poet's image has in fact been truly derived from its corresponding Idea, Sidney simply replies: "that the Poet hath that *Idea* is manifest, by deliuering them forth in such excellencie as hee hath imagined them" (p. 157). For Sidney, one knows an Idea is there by a kind of intuitive recognition; no further reflection is necessary. For Temple, by contrast, relations between images and Ideas cannot simply be intuited, because while invention can certainly lead one to true universals, and from there to true fictions, it can mislead as well. Only if Ideas have been derived by the proper precepts of rational thought — the rules of dialectic — can one be assured of their truth.

In this criticism of Sidney's definition, the reasons why Temple feels Sidney to have slighted logic's role in mediating between image and Idea are not fully explicit. The same issue arises, however, when Sidney defends poetry against the charge of lying, and there Temple explains his position on poetic truth more fully. To refute the lying charge, Sidney proceeds much as he does in defining poetry, first pointing to the ties other arts have to reality, then describing poetry's freedom: "of all Writers vnder the sunne, the Poet is the least lier ..." (p. 184). "[T]o lye," Sydney explains, "is to affirme that to be true which is false." Other artists, "affirming many things, can, in the cloudy knowledge of mankinde, hardly escape from many lyes," but "for the Poet, he nothing affirmes, and therefore neuer lyeth" (p. 184).

This argument is beautifully made, but it is in a crucial sense incomplete. Sidney addresses the truth of the relation words hold between a poetic representation and the world, yet as different scholars have pointed out, that is not the truth relation that poetry's sophisticated critics have in mind.[25] Ascham's complaint about romances and "Italianate books," for example, is not that they tell of things that never happened, but rather that they show in both example and precept how to act ill. They lie in their representations of the ideal, not in their representations of nature.[26] Even Gosson, whose *School of Abuse* is often taken as the immediate cause for this passage in the *Apology*, avoids the literal lying charge. Instead he attacks poetry for its ability to insinuate true-seeming but still immoral principles which, by the same powers of moving that Sidney elevates as poetry's great virtue, rapt listeners will think excellent and imitable. "Cookes did never shew more crafte in their junckets to vanquish the taste, nor Painteres in shadows to allure the eye, then poets in theaters to wounde the conscience." Cooks and painters merely deceive the senses, but poets, "by the private entrys of the eare, slip downe into the hart, and with gunshotte of affection gaule the minde, where reason and vertue should rule the roste."[27]

Such a remark reveals in Sidney's argument a self-defeating irony. For however neatly Sidney's poet-not-affirming-and-thence-not-lying argument parries the literal lie attack, to the more sophisticated charge that poets lie because they give us images that misrepresent ideal virtue, Sidney's argument actually weakens his own case for poetry's value. To argue that poets do not affirm may protect poets from charges that they lie, but it also forecloses the claim that one of poetry's strengths is its capacity for teaching truth. If the poet does not affirm things as true, then what are we to say about universal Ideas? Does the poet not in some manner affirm them? Does he not hold them for true and is that not in fact the basic moral justification for poetry? Sidney has worked himself into a dilemma. If the poet does not affirm, he cannot be said to lie; but unless the poet affirms, he cannot be said to tell truth. Temple wants to say that poets do indeed affirm truth, and his comments thus try to establish two different senses of truth-telling.

Temple's response to Sidney's dilemma begins by questioning Sidney's definition of a lie. Sidney says that to lie is to affirm something which is false to be true, but by "affirm" Sidney seems to mean something more than simply "say." Temple distrusts this. Suppose someone should say, "Man is not an animal." Is this a lie? "You will perhaps reply that you agree this axiom has been negated and is false, but nevertheless that it is not lying, if someone makes a statement this way, negating arguments that (as it were) agree with each other in his mind, unless he should also affirm through a new mental act, i.e., a further statement, that this false axiom is true" (p. 137). As Temple understands Sidney, to say "Man is not an animal" can only be a lie if the speaker not only utters the axiom but also "affirms" it, and this in turn seems to imply not just that the speaker must make the original statement, but that he must also add some sort of affirmation to show that the statement is to be taken for true. This extra statement — "and this is true," or "I believe it" — Temple describes as an argument from testimony, or an argument which testifies to the speaker's experience, rather than one derived solely from logical inferences from first principles. But Temple is impatient with the thought that such an extra, "adventitious" affirmation is necessary before one can be said to have lied. For him, a lie is to be judged simply by whether the proposition in question has been properly derived "in accord with the precepts of logic." "Just as an axiom [i.e., statement] is true when it states how the nature of the matter stands, similarly, that axiom will be false and lying when it states something that does not agree with the nature of the matter, even if an affirmation of the mind is not added on" (p137).

In an important way Temple seems here at a disadvantage. Surely, in ordinary usage if one utters a falsehood while thinking it true, one has not "lied;" but Temple sees this as the only way to avoid Sidney's dilemma about telling truth: "if there is no lie except by our affirmation ... then certainly truth will not exist, if you do not bring both mental assent and testimony to proving or disproving the sense of this further statement. But truth does not depend upon this mental assent and testimony; instead it arises from the [true] nature of things and from disposition" (p. 137). After all, one does not need facts drawn from experience to evaluate conceptually derived truths. Such truths are deduced from *a priori* principles through logical precepts, and thus even in the absence of arguments from experience, "the essence of truth can still be established." Finally, having set up the truth problem such that he can both agree and disagree with Sidney's assertion that the poet affirms nothing, Temple concludes: "that [assertion] is certainly true, if we are thinking not of an affirmation that arises from the amicable assembling, as it were, of one argument with another, but rather of that affirmation that has the force of testimony to making that further truth-claim. But if you consider that first kind of affirmation, poetry is rich in the affirmation of axioms" (p. 137).

Temple's division of the truth/lying problem into two kinds of affirmation not only allows the defense that poetry does not "lie" when a London company puts on a show set in Rome, but it also allows both for affirmations of universal truths, and for a way of guaranteeing their truth. Poets are not off merely "making up" things disconnected to any sort of reality, unverifiable except by insight; instead they are imagining rationally and intelligibly, and their imaginations are neither any more likely to lie than anyone else's, nor any less subject to correction when they do.

In both the arguments discussed so far, Temple's objections show him to be emphasizing problems of understanding which he feels Sidney has slighted. In responding to one other major passage in the *Apology* he extends the emphasis on conceptual issues, but this time in disagreement with Sidney over the value to be placed on poetry's power to move. Sidney's argument in this section is that poetry has a special capacity to bring men to virtuous action. Even if it were true, Sidney suggests, that the philosopher actually teaches better than the poet, still the poet has the more important power of moving men to action. "[M]oouing," Sidney argues, "is of a higher degree then teaching," and this is true because moving "is wel nigh the cause and the effect of teaching" (p. 171). Of what use is teaching if one is not also moved to action? Teaching may be good, "but to be moued to doe that which we know, or to be mooued with desire to knowe, *Hoc opus, hic labor est"* (p. 172). Because moving first causes us to learn and then causes us to act upon what we have learned, and because poetry moves men more powerfully than any other art, the poet (Sidney tells us again) is "the Monarch" "of all Sciences."

In response to this argument, Temple focuses on Sidney's exposition of the causal relation between moving and teaching. As usual, Temple outlines the syllogistic form of Sidney's argument in order to isolate its premises for judgment:

Proposition: The cause and the effect of teaching are of a higher degree than teaching itself.
Assumption: Moving is the cause and the effect of teaching.
Conclusion: Moving, therefore, is of a higher degree than teaching itself. (p. 115)

The argument set out, Temple then voices objections to both premises, but his important complaint concerns the Assumption. Moving, he tells Sidney, is not properly speaking a "cause" of teaching at all, and therefore moving cannot be said to excel teaching. "Certainly you will never be taught just by moving; yet that would be the case if moving were the cause of teaching. We are only taught by that which brings about some sort of knowledge in the mind; yet this does not happen by any 'moving,' but only by the force and illumination of an argument, ordered through the rules of judgment" (p. 115). As Temple continues, he takes pains to point out that Sidney's use of the term "cause" has in this argument two distinct senses. In the first of these, the "cause" of learning (or of "being taught") is "what urges or attracts us to learning;" but in its other sense, the "cause" of learning is that force "by which knowledge is begotten and formed, as it were, in someone's mind" (p. 117). Temple will agree that "moving" may make one want to learn — will be a cause in the first sense — but he will not agree that moving can cause the conceptual process of learning itself. That is a matter of understanding, not of will. "Keep the issue of 'moving' distinct from that of arguments," he tells Sidney. Even if poetry does move men better than any other discipline, that will not bear on the issue of whether poetry surpasses other arts. Moreover, since it is the force and illumination of argument which is the true conceptual cause of learning, then whenever learning something leads to action, it will necessarily be the force and illumination of argument that is the ultimate cause. "Observe, then, that if you set this syllogism of yours out properly, moving is not so much to be valued above the act of teaching, as the act of teaching is to be valued above moving..." (p. 115). And finally, even granting that poetry is causal in the sense that it can make us want to be taught, still "we are also attracted to learning through the making of arguments and through eloquence" (p. 117). Not just poetry, but logic and rhetoric as well can move men to want to know. To the extent that it moves us to learn, poetry is to be valued neither more nor less than other arts; and to the extent it teaches, it does so through the logical processes of forceful reasoning.

In this section, then, as in his response to Sidney's definition of poetry, Temple thinks Sidney slights problems inherent in knowing, and thereby exaggerates poetry's position among the arts. Sidney's aesthetic for Temple simply does not place enough importance on the conceptual problems of understanding. Though Sidney includes "teaching" in his definition of poetry, and though he speaks of poetry's capacity to entertain "the diuine consideration of what can and should be," he nevertheless seems unconcerned that prior questions of what one teaches or how one knows should themselves raise difficulties. In Sidney's view we know what perfection is; the problem is our failure to pursue it. Temple by contrast is willing to grant poetry a power to move us to action, but his concern is in what precedes moving. Thus he keeps reminding Sidney of problems of knowing, learning and inventing, and through these "logical" issues he repeatedly suggests his sense that the formulation of an aesthetic must begin not with will, but with understanding.

In the three replies I have outlined so far, Temple's aim is to argue for poetry's logical character, to place poetry together with the other humanist arts of discourse as a vehicle of reason and teaching. But beyond their emphasis on understanding as opposed to will, implicit in each of these objections is Temple's basic strategy with respect to the defense of poetry: where Sidney argues that poetry is essentially different from all other arts, Temple insists that it is to be valued for what it shares with those arts. In other passages from the *Analysis* this difference in strategy is made more clear; in a series of replies to Sidney's attacks on other disciplines, Temple patiently counters Sidney's claims for poetry's dominance, always defending against what he takes to be overstated criticisms of the competing arts. When, for example, Sidney says that the moral philosopher, "setting downe with thorny argument the bare rule" is "hard of vtterance" because "his knowledge standeth so vpon the abstract and generall that happie is the man who may vnderstande him" (p. 164), Temple replies that though this sort of obscurity may be a fault in particular philosophers, it is not a fault in the art itself. "For rightly described and set out in all its parts, ethics contains not only precepts but examples as well, through which we should be instructed how to achieve felicity" (p. 99). And as for the obscurity that comes from the abstract and general consideration of things, this, Temple argues, "is no more fittingly argued against ethics than against poetry and other arts whose precepts deal with any general thing" (p. 101). This same line of reply comes up later in an aside when Sidney argues that poetry is "more Philosophicall and more studiously serious then history" because it deals "with the vniuersall consideration" (p. 167):

> Earlier, ethics was accused of a certain obscurity because it is made up of universal notions. But here, the poet, because he considers things universally, and not singularly in species, is said for that reason to be more suited for teaching than the historian. But if considering things through universals is to be approved of in the poet, it ought not to be condemned in a teacher of ethics. (p. 107)

But it is not just the philosopher Temple defends. To Sidney's argument that history, "beeing captiued to the trueth of a foolish world, is many times a terror from well dooing, and an incouragement to vnbrideled wickednes" (p. 170), thus actually discouraging virtue and encouraging vice, Temple replies that poetry is as vulnerable to this argument as is history: "Through this same argument (most noble Sidney) you can criticize comedy and tragedy, and even Homer's *Odyssey*, where Ulysses, a man of excellent virtue, is afflicted with several sorts of calamities" (p. 113). At another point, Temple argues against Sidney with the converse. When Sidney argues in defense of comedy that its representations of vice are to be sanctioned because they teach us to hate the vice we see, Temple observes: "the same things you use to defend comedy . . . can in turn be very nicely transferred to the defense of history. To the extent you wound history in one argument, you heal the wound in another. And the historian will deny absolutely that the poet is the only author of such notable learning" (p. 111)

It is not necessary here to review all of Temple's remarks; these are representative. In all he says, Temple stresses both the rationality of poetry, and its common enterprise with ethics, history and the other arts. Though at no point does he deny to poetry qualities Sidney confers upon it, he consistently opposes describing as essential to poetry alone such tasks as teaching, or delighting, or the making of "true" fictions. Unlike Sidney, who would define poetry by singling out its inimitable character as necessary to a well-lived life, Temple is content to defend poetry as but an art among arts—no better, and no worse.

We have no idea of Sidney's response to Temple's comments. Even had Sidney agreed with Temple that in a strict sense his theories could be improved, because Sidney's aesthetic does not place the same value Temple's does on conceptual issues, there is reason to doubt that he would ever have rewritten a word. As C. S. Lewis has written of Sidney, "If poetry does not ravish, it is for him nothing. The 'golden world' it presents must be set forth 'in so rich Tapistry' as Nature never knew, must lure us into itself."[28] But beyond the issues of wit and will, there is perhaps an even more fundamental reason Sidney is likely to have laid Temple's advice aside. For Sidney's arguments in the *Apology* are often not "arguments" at all. Rather they are positions taken, volleys fired, in a war that has less to do with the defense of poetry than with the declaration of its independence. When one thinks about it, after all, what sort of "defense" can this be when the bulk of one's text is devoted to offending the very people who most need convincing? Anywhere one looks in the *Analysis*, the practitioners of every art are instructed in their inferiority. The philosopher is dull, the historian encourages vice as often as virtue, the lawyer cares only about his particular case and never about the public weal. And as for the astronomer, the musician, and the mathematician, each of these is but a player in a drama of another's inspiration. Instead of a defense, Sidney seems more concerned to write a credo. England's "new poets," as Spenser's E. K. calls them,[29] do not need to be told that they are brothers and sisters to everybody else. Instead they need an energizing voice which can assure them of poetry's value, and which can thereby establish a sense of community and common cause among an otherwise small and threatened band.

Whatever theoretical disputes Temple raises with Sidney, then, and however even-handed Temple's own strategy to defend poetry might have been, the interest of Temple's text will finally be independent of whether Sidney or Temple on any given issue is "right." Temple's remarks are as close as we will ever come to seeing how educated Tudor readers actually responded to Sidney's work; they also show better than any other document we have that the kind of close, hard reading that must always underlie literary argument was already very much a part of the English critical tradition. But along with these pragmatic concerns, Temple's *Analysis* testifies to a wider and more vigorous range of debate in Tudor literary circles than can be gleaned from the *Apology* alone. The brilliance of Sidney's work may at times make us think of Sidney's as the only possible Tudor aesthetic; Temple's positions

remind us it was not. Temple reads Sidney as a modern critic hopes
to read other modern critics: to agree, to disagree, to improve by
judicious comment, to locate something near the "truth." Like other
Elizabethans, Temple had his own theories of poetry, and to him the
Apology — however well done — nevertheless represented but one of the
aesthetic positions among which any serious reader had to find a
place.[30]

III

Temple's Life

Sir William Temple (1555-1627) lived a life close to the humanist
scholar-courtier dream.[31] Early in his career his scholarly achievements
brought him to the edges of political power, and even when events
made preferment possible only in Ireland, he remained politically as
well as academically active. Educated at Eton, Temple entered King's
College, Cambridge, as a scholarship student in 1573. He was elected
a fellow in 1576, graduated BA in 1577-78, and MA in 1581. At Cambridge he developed his interest in philosophy and logic, and in 1580
entered into a short pamphlet war with the Oxford logician Everard
Digby over the merits of Ramus' Method.[32] Temple left Cambridge
in 1584 to become master of the Lincoln Grammar school; in the same
year he published *P. Rami Dialecticae libri duo scholiis G. Tempelli Can-
tabrigiensis illustrati,* the most complete and careful of the English Ramist
logics. The book also has the distinction of being remembered as the
first book printed by the Cambridge University press.

Temple dedicated the *Dialecticae* to Sir Philip Sidney, sending Sidney
a copy early in 1584. Sidney's letter in response has been preserved,
and it makes clear his appreciation for Temple's work:

Good Mr Temple. I have receaved both yowr book and letter,
and think my self greatly beholding unto yow for them. I greatly desyre to know yow better, I mean by sight, for els yowr
wrytings make yow as well known as my knowledg ever reach
unto, and this assure yourself Mr Temple that whyle I live yow
shall have me reddy to make known by my best power that I
bear yow good will, and greatly esteem those thinges I conceav

in yow. When yow com to London or Court I prai yow lett me
see yow, mean whyle use me boldli: for I am beholding. God
keep yow well. At Court this 23th of Mai 1584.

> Your loving frend
> Philip Sidnei

To my assured good frend
Mr William Temple[33]

Temple accepted Sidney's invitation and the two seem to have gotten
along just as well as the tone of Sidney's letter implies they might. Temple became Sidney's secretary in November, 1585, when Sidney was
appointed governor to Flushing. He served Sidney in this office until
Sidney's death; Sidney is said to have died in Temple's arms. Temple
is mentioned in Sidney's will, being left an annuity of thirty pounds.

After Sidney's death in 1586, Temple served a series of court-related
masters. He worked first for William Davison, the queen's secretary,
then for Sir Thomas Smith, clerk of the Privy Council, and finally
for Robert Devereux, the second earl of Essex. He served Essex from
1594 to 1601, when Essex's rebellion left him, along with many others,
very much out of favor. Though Temple protested his ignorance of
Essex's plot to overthrow Elizabeth, Sir Robert Cecil seems not to have
been convinced. Given both that Temple was elected in 1597 to the
House of Commons through Essex's influence, and that he probably
accompanied Essex to Ireland in 1599, the relationship between Temple and Essex seems to have been close enough that Cecil's suspicions
are understandable. In any case, though no proceedings were taken
against him, for some years Temple was unable to get advancement.
Bacon, who had also served Essex, seems in 1605 to have tried to have
Temple knighted, but this effort was unsuccessful. Finally, in 1609
Temple was offered the post of provost of Trinity College, Dublin,
where he then served until his death in January, 1627. In Dublin, Temple was a man of some importance. He was appointed a master in
chancery in 1610, and elected the member for Dublin University in
the Irish House of Commons in 1614. He was knighted in 1622 at
the age of sixty-seven.

In addition to the *Analysis*, the edition of Ramus' *Dialectic*, and the
various disputations with Digby over Ramist Method, Temple's written work includes two other volumes of analysis: *A Logicall Analysis
of Twentye Select Psalmes performed by W. Temple* (London, 1605), and
the longer Latin version, *Analysis logica triginta psalmorum* (London,
1611). The English *Analysis*, dedicated to the young Prince of Wales,
was probably part of Temple's effort to regain favor. Like the *Analysis*

of the *Apology*, these works show careful line-by-line attention to text. Unlike the Sidney analysis, however, the Psalms analyses include no literary commentary or argumentation.

The Text of Temple's "Analysis"

As copy text for this edition I have used the American Council of Learned Societies British Manuscript Project microfilm of the single manuscript copy owned by the Viscount De L'Isle, printed here with the very kind permission of Lord De L'Isle. Temple's MS is listed in *H M C De L'Isle and Dudley*, 1, 1925, p. 304, no. 1095 (BMP checklist reference: J 375, no. 1095, Camb. 785/2-6). Despite Lord De L'Isle's kind efforts to search it out, the manuscript cannot now be located. A photographic copy of Temple's Latin text has also been transcribed by Professor William A. Elwood, as an appendix to his doctoral dissertation edition of Sidney's *Defense* (University of Chicago, 1967). Professor Elwood has graciously provided me with a copy of his transcription, and mine has profited from double-checking against his.

The microfilm indicates an octavo-sized volume of forty leaves— twenty sheets folded and tied with ribbon.[34] The text is unpaginated and unfoliated. The first and last folio leaves, [1-1v; 40-40v], act as a protective outer covering and are filled with an unrelated Latin text in Gothic script. In the bottom margin of [1] is the title: *"Analysis tractationis de Poesi contextae a nobilissimo viro Philippe Sydneio."* The collation of the entire MS is as follows: [1-1v] unrelated Latin text, with title of Temple's MS in lower margin of [1]; [2-2v] blank; [3] coat of arms; [3v-5] blank; [5v] dedicatory poem; [6-38v] text; [39-39v] blank; [40-40v] unrelated Latin text. The manuscript is written in two distinct hands: Hand A is responsible for the text from [5v-31], and from [36v-38v]; Hand B is responsible for the title on [1] and for the text from [31v-36]. Hand A is probably Temple's own. It is a clearly legible italic script, with some secretary features, and shows very close similarity to his autograph in B. L. *Egerton MS.* 1239, f. 64. Hand B is fully italic, very even and precise, its script somewhat larger than that of Hand A.

Format

The most difficult problem in editing Temple's text is his format. Ramist analyses often favored outline forms, and Temple's provides an excellent example of how such spatial organization was used.

Temple employs two kinds of paragraphing: the block paragraph, in which all lines share the same left margin; and (by far the most common) what is now called the "hang-indented" paragraph. In these paragraphs, the ordinary conventions of modern prose paragraphing are reversed, such that the first line begins at the margin, and all subsequent lines are indented. To indicate subordination, Temple then arranges these hang-indented paragraphs hierarchically. This arrangement, combined with interlinear spacings to indicate shifts in analytical focus, give Temple's logical structure a spatially realized representation. Especially because the process of spatialization is itself an interesting issue in the intellectual history of the sixteenth century, I have preserved Temple's format as far as possible.

In general, Temple's format conventions are clear and consistent. At the same time, there are still many variations in Temple's procedures, and these have been dealt with in different ways. To begin with, the largest number of Temple's inconsistencies are not so much errors or inattentions as they are reflections of what seems to be a basic disinclination to rationalize his procedures fully. While, for example, Temple often indents to exemplify comparisons, he does not always do so; similarly, Temple varies considerably his use of interlinear spacings. Since inconsistencies of this kind bear on the question of just how seriously attentive to system Temple actually was, and since regularizing these variations would suggest a much more rigorous formalizing than Temple in fact shows, these inconsistencies have been left unchanged. But though most of Temple's variations in format fall into this class of "countenanced" inconsistencies, there are others which I have thought it best to regularize. Of these, the first are those which clearly result from lapses of attention in copying. These occur when the copyist moves from one folio leaf to the next, and in doing so loses track of his level of indentation. Inconsistencies of this sort have been silently regularized. Second, though Temple is never unclear about how he intends his hierarchical relations to be construed, he does vary the depth of the indentations he uses to establish subparagraphs and sub-subparagraphs. All such variations in the depth of indentation have also been silently regularized. Finally, there are a small number of cases where an inconsistency occurs which is not obviously attributable to mis-copying, but which is also so unlike Temple's usual practice that it is almost undoubtedly an unintended error. In these cases I have emended Temple's format, and noted the change in the text.

Text

Temple's text is, on the whole, legible and largely free of errors;

the nature of the corrections which do occur suggest the manuscript to be a carefully proofread fair copy. This edition makes use of the following conventions:

Cancellations: All cancellations which indicate changes of wording are retained in pointed brackets: ⟨*tractatur*⟩. Minor scribal errors of inadvertent repetition have been silently deleted.

Scribal Insertions: The few words which the copyists have inserted above the line are indicated by half brackets: ⌐*est*¬.

Contractions and Abbreviations: I have silently expanded contractions for the genitive and ablative/dative plurals, for passive endings, for *m* and *n*, for *pro-/prae-*, for digraphs, and (in Hand B) for nouns ending in *-us*. Abbreviations, on the other hand, have not been expanded. While spellings have not been regularized, ornamental initials and the old long *s* have been silently modernized.

Emendations: Emendations have been made for words which have been miswritten, and, on two occasions, for punctuation. All have been noted in the text.

Editorial Interpolations: Because of the way in which the ribbon has been used to bind the text, there are points at which the very end of lines at the right-hand margin of verso leaves is hidden from the camera. Where this has occured, I have interpolated the missing text. These interpolations consist of one, occasionally two, letters, and end line punctuation. Interpolations have also been made for words and punctuation too faint to read, and for blotted words. All of these interpolations have been indicated by square brackets: [mihi]. Finally, any missing or invisible full-stop which Temple's practice would require at the end of citations or after abbreviations has been inserted silently.

Sidney's English: Where Temple quotes Sidney's English, I have rendered him exactly. Though Temple's references are frequent, they are so brief that they have little or no textual authority. In any event, only a few of these quotations vary from either the early printed versions by Ponsonby or Olney (P and O), or from the two extant manuscripts at Norwich (N) and Penshurst (Pe). I have noted where Temple's quotations differ substantially from the other texts. For discussion of the relative merits of Olney, Ponsonby, and the extant manuscripts, see Katherine Duncan-Jones and Jan A. van

Dorsten, eds., *Miscellaneous Prose of Sir Philip Sidney* (Oxford: Clarendon Press, 1973), pp. 65-70.

Translation

The translation follows the layout of the Latin original, except that
I have added paragraphing within some of Temple's long commen-
tary/responses to Sidney's positions. The translation keeps close to the
Latin, though in the interest of readability I have not hesitated to
substitute active for passive forms, to supply antecedents, or to ex-
pand jargon phrases whose meanings would otherwise seem obscure.
In the frequent places where Temple's Latin is a direct translation of
Sidney's English, I have usually tried to use Sidney to render Temple. Where, however, Temple's Latin reveals a distinctly different
understanding of Sidney's meaning than modern readers would expect, I have rendered Temple literally. The more interesting of these
cases have been noted (see for example Translation Note 22). I have
also expanded Temple's references to the *Apology*, since the sense of
his analysis is often incomplete without the full passage in the *Apology*
to which he refers. I have taken the expansions from G. Gregory
Smith's *Elizabethan Critical Essays* (Oxford: Oxford University Press,
1904), 1: 150-207, and I have noted page numbers in parentheses
following the quotations. I use Smith, who follows Olney's edition of
the *Apology*, because his is the most available unmodernized text.

Finally a word about two difficulties in reading the *Analysis*. First,
Temple's work is very closely keyed to Sidney's text, and even with
all of the references Temple includes to specific passages, his descriptions often make full sense only when read with the *Apology* itself. I
have inserted especially crucial lines wherever possible, either bracketed
in the text or in a note, but most readers will profit from having Sidney's
text directly at hand while reading Temple. Second, Temple uses the
terminology of the Renaissance logician-rhetorician. This has its
usefulness in giving concrete illustration of how those terms of art were
used, but it can also be confusing. Terms like "argument," "axiom,"
and "method" all have meanings different from current usage, and even
with the explanations supplied in the first part of this introduction,
few modern readers will feel as at home with adjuncts, disparates and
effects as the Elizabethan students who spent hours of drill in these
matters. To help with this jargon I include the following glossary; an
early familiarity with Tudor logical terminology may allow readers
to preserve more easily their patience with Temple's often rather
technical prose.

Glossary

Adjunct: A quality or circumstance of a subject. In the axiom "Poetry is ancient," "ancient" names an adjunct of poetry.

Antecedent: The first axiom, or premise, of an enthymeme. See Enthymeme.

Apodosis: The second term of a comparison. The first term is called the "protasis." See the example at Protasis.

Argument: 1) Any simple term, e.g., in the axiom "Man is an animal," there are two arguments, "man," and "animal." 2) A persuasive demonstration (the modern sense of the word).

Assumption: The second axiom, or premise, of a syllogism. See Syllogism.

Axiom (Latin, *axioma*, or *enuntiatum*): a proposition, or assertion, e.g., "God created man," "The cat is on the mat." Axiom does *not* suggest its modern sense of maxim or first principle.

Cause: Temple takes his doctrine of causes from Aristotelian tradition, where there were four kinds of causes: efficient, final, material, and formal. The *efficient* (or "procreant") *cause* is the agent or force which produces something; the *final cause* is the end, or purpose, which something is designed to serve; the *material cause* is the matter of which something is made; and the *formal cause* is the defining conception or design towards which a thing is shaped. Thus in the case of a bronze cup, the efficient cause would be the craftsman; the final cause, to hold water for drinking; the material cause, bronze; the formal cause, the craftsman's abstract conception of the cup's form towards which he shapes his material. Aristotle's most concise treatment of these causes is *Metaphysics* Δ. 2, 1013a24–5.

Comparison (*comparatio, collocatio*): Comparisons are either by quality or by quantity. By quantity, a thing compared can be either equal to something else, less than something else, or greater than something else. Thus the terms "Comparison from the equal," "Comparison from the lesser," and "Comparison from the greater" (*e pari, e minore, e majore*).

Comparison by quality compares objects either with respect to likeness or to unlikeness. A "Comparison of likes" can also be termed a "Simile"; a "Comparison of unlikes" can be termed a "Dissimile." The first term of any comparison is called the Protasis; the second term is the Apodosis.

Conclusion: What is deduced from the premises of a syllogism. The third axiom of a syllogism. See Syllogism.

Conjugates: Words which share the same root, but have different affixes: e.g., "free," "freely," "freedom"; or "teach," "teaching."

Consequent: The second term, or conclusion of an enthymeme. An enthymeme's first term is the Antecedent. See Enthymeme.

Crypsis: A deliberate inversion (or "hiding") of Method in the ordering of arguments. Crypsis is a rhetorical strategy that is properly used, Temple explains, "when we want to delight, move, or deceive" an audience (*Dialecticae*, p. 144).

Differences (*diversa*): Attributes which contrast and are to be distinguished in a particular subject, but not because they are logically opposed. To say "Ulysses was not handsome, but eloquent," is to argue from differences, since it is logically possible that Ulysses could be both handsome and eloquent. Compare Disparates.

Disparates: Attributes which are opposed and necessarily inconsistent. The axiom "Alcibiades cannot be both white and black in the same part of his body" argues from disparates. Compare Differences.

Disposition: The second part of logic, also called Judgment. It is concerned with the ordering, or "disposing," of arguments and axioms. See Judgment.

Distribution: A division of a class into its subordinate parts or kinds. Sidney distributes poets into three kinds: divine poets, philosophical poets, and right poets.

Effect: Anything that has been caused. Though humanist logics usually define four types of effect, corresponding to the four types of cause, in the *Analysis* Temple does not bother to distinguish between these different effects. See Cause.

Efficient cause: The agent or force which produces something. God is the efficient cause of man. See Cause.

Enthymeme: A syllogism in which one of the premises is not made explicit. The first term of an enthymeme is called the Antecedent, the second is called the Consequent:

Antecedent: Poets are called *Vates* and *poeta*.
Consequent: Poets are therefore to be praised.
What is omitted in this example is the implicit major premise: "Those who are called *Vates* and *poeta* are to be praised."

Equal (i.e., a *Comparison of Equals*): A comparison of quantity. See Comparison.

Final cause: The end or purpose for which something is designed. Drinking is the final cause of a cup. See Cause.

Genus: A general classification for individuals related by kind. "Animal" is a genus for both "man" and "lion." Conversely, "man" and "lion" are "species" with respect to the genus "animal."

Greater (i.e., *Comparison from the greater*): A comparison of quantity. See Comparison.

Induction: A mode of argument which justifies its conclusion by enumeration. The following is an induction of specials:

The poetry of Musaeus, Homer, Hesiod, Orpheus, Linus is older than all other disciplines;

Poetry is therefore the oldest discipline.

Invention: The first part of logic. Invention concerns how one finds or classifies arguments from which axioms can be constructed. See Introduction, part 1.

Judgment: The second part of logic, also called "Disposition." The tasks of Judgment are first, to arrange terms into axioms; second, to test axioms (if need be) through syllogism; and third, to use the rules of Method to order axioms into large-scale discourse. See Introduction, part 1.

Kathauto: In accord with the Law of Justice. See Laws of Truth, Justice, and Wisdom.

Katholou proton: In accord with the Law of Wisdom. See Laws of Truth, Justice, and Wisdom.

Laws of Truth, Justice, and Wisdom: In his discussion of axiomatical judgment Ramus proposes three laws by which axioms may be tested to determine whether they can be included as true and necessary precepts of an art. These are the Law of Truth (also *lex de omni*), the Law of Justice (also *lex homogenii*), and the Law of Wisdom (*lex catholici*). Temple uses two of these laws in the *Analysis*, the Law of Justice, for which he uses the Greek term *kathauto*, and the Law of Wisdom, for which he uses the term *katholou proton*.

The Law of Truth (*de omni*) requires that axioms be true in all cases, i.e., that they be necessary and not contingent. This law is designed to keep matters of opinion, where the axiom in question may or may not be true, out of "scientific" matters. Scientific axioms should be true in all cases, e.g., "A triangle has three sides."

The Law of Justice (Temple's *kathauto*) requires that the arguments of an axiom be fully "homogenous" — they must fit together in an

essential way, as the formal cause with the form it causes, or a subject with its proper adjunct. The technical meaning of this law is
complicated, but its aim is simply to sort out which matters belong
"essentially" to each of the different arts, and thus to establish clear
boundaries between arts and to eliminate redundancies. Where, for
example, both logic and rhetoric had traditionally treated Invention, Ramus' Law of Justice required a decision as to which of these
arts best agreed with Invention in its essential subject matter.
Because Invention depends on reason, and because Ramus described
the essential matter of logic as natural reasoning, Ramus classed
Invention with logic. The essential matter of rhetoric, on the other
hand, was the forceful ornamentation of speech, and because this
is not the essence of Invention, rhetoric and Invention are not
homogenous. For rhetoric to treat Invention, Ramus argued, thus
only creates redundancy while confusing the essential characters of
logic and rhetoric.

Finally, the Law of Wisdom, Temple's *katholou proton*, requires
that the subject term and predicate term of an axiom do not operate
on different levels of generality. W. S. Howell paraphrases Roland
MacIlmaine's explanation of this law as follows: "If I ask what logic
is . . . and you reply that it teaches how to invent arguments," your
answer is not in accord with the Law of Wisdom "for you have treated
a general thing particularly. 'I aske the . . . for the definition of the
whole arte, and thow geuest me the definition of inuention, which
is but part of the arte' " (*Logic and Rhetoric*, p. 182). Logic does teach
how to invent arguments, but it also teaches other things as well,
and thus to say only that "logic teaches how to invent arguments"
misleads by using a predicate that is not general enough to match
its subject.

In brief: when Temple says that something is not *kathauto*, he
means it mixes disciplines; when he says that something is not *katholou
proton*, he means that one of the axiom's terms is too general for the
other. (For more discussion of these laws, see Temple's *Dialecticae*,
pp. 73–82; Fraunce, *LL*, 87b–90a; and Howell, pp. 149–53, 181–83.)

Lesser (*Comparison from the lesser*): A comparison of quantity. See
Comparison.

Like (*Comparison of likes*): A comparison of quality, a simile. See
Comparison.

Material cause: The matter from which something is made. The material
cause of Man is clay. See Cause.

Method: That part of logic which deals with organizing axioms into large-scale discourse. The main principle of Method is that in organizing a set of axioms one begins with the most general of them and proceeds by degrees to the most specific. Any deviation from this order is a "crypsis" of Method. See Introduction, part I.

Notation: An argument drawn from etymology. Antony Wotton's *Art of Logic* (London, 1626) cites Spenser's *Faerie Queene*, 6.1.1. as an example of an argument drawn from notation: "Of court it seemes men courtesie do call."

Place (locus): Any of the different categories of argument set out in Invention: e.g., cause, effect, subject, adjunct, differences, disparates, comparison. A seat of argument, a topic.

Prolepsis: An objection a speaker raises against his own argument, in order to answer it before an opponent can make use of it.

Proposition: 1) The first axiom (major premise) of a syllogism (see Syllogism). 2) An alternative term for Protasis, the first term of a comparison.

Prosyllogism: An argument or illustration which supports any of the three axioms of a syllogism. A prosyllogism is often itself a syllogism whose conclusion provides the major or minor premise to its head syllogism.

Protasis: The first term of a comparison. The second term is the Apodosis.

> Protasis: As in geometry the oblique must bee knowne as wel as the right;
>
> Apodosis: So in the actions of our life who seeth not the filthiness of evil wanteth a great foile to perceive the beauty of vertue. (*Apology*, p. 177).

Reddition: The second term of a comparison; more usually, Apodosis.

Relatives: Terms dealing with logically opposed members of the same class: "father" and "son" are relatives, as are "teaching" and "learning," or "cause" and "effect."

Special: Any particular example of a general, or universal, term. Of the general class "philosophers," Plato and Aristotle are specials.

Species: A member of a genus. "Man" is a species of the genus "animal."

Subject: That to which adjuncts belong. "Poetry" is a subject to the adjuncts of antiquity and commonality among all nations. "Man" is a subject to which rationality is an adjunct.

Syllogism: Abraham Fraunce defines syllogism as "a disposition of thre axiomes, wherbie or wherin a doubtfull question . . . is necessarily concluded and determined" (*SL*, p. 147). The three axioms are called the Proposition (the major premise), the Assumption (the minor premise), and the Conclusion. There are two main classes of syllogism in Ramist logic, the simple and the compound. Simple syllogisms are made up of syntactically simple axioms (e.g., "Socrates is mortal"); compound syllogisms include a conjoined, or compound axiom in the Proposition (e.g., "If Socrates is a man, then he is mortal").

Simple syllogisms: Because each of the three simple axioms in these syllogisms has two terms — a subject and a predicate — and because a complete syllogism will see each single term appear twice — once in each of two axioms — there will always be a total of just three different terms distributed throughout the form. An example:

Proposition: Socrates is a man.
Assumption: A man is mortal.
Conclusion: Therefore, Socrates is mortal.

The three terms here are "Socrates," "man," and "mortal." Of these terms, the two which make up the Conclusion (i.e., "Socrates" and "mortal") are called the "extremes," and the other term ("man"), which is common to both premises but which does not occur in the Conclusion, is called the "mean," or "middle," or "third" term. As Fraunce gently explains the theory of all this: "The necessitye of the consequence in a syllogisme dependeth òn that ould grounde, that suche thinges as agre in any third thinge, must also agre among themselves" (*SL*, p. 149). The forms of the syllogism are intended to give all the valid ways of using this middle term to show the necessary agreement of the extremes.

Simple syllogisms are classified by where the middle term occurs in the premises. There are three such classes in Ramus: the *contracted syllogism*, the *full syllogism of the first figure*, and the *full syllogism of the second figure*.

The *contracted syllogism*, despite its name, need not in fact be contracted, though in discourse it very often is. When it is set out in all its parts, its middle term supplies the subject for both the major and the minor premises:

Proposition: Socrates is a philosopher.
Assumption: Socrates is a Greek.
Conclusion: Therefore, some philosophers are Greek.

The special character of this "figure" (as the different forms of the syllogism are called) is that it can be contracted to appear as just a conclusion and an accompanying example: "Some philosophers are Greek, as Socrates." Here, though the premises are not explicit, they are nevertheless implied.

The *full syllogism of the first figure* is characterized by having its middle term serve as the predicate in both premises, and by having this middle term negated in one of the premises. The Conclusion is also negated:

Proposition: A good shepherd is not idle.

Assumption: Paris is idle.

Conclusion: Therefore, Paris is not a good shepherd.

The *full syllogism of the second figure* is characterized by having its middle term serve as the subject in the Proposition, and as the predicate in the Assumption:

Proposition: A thing which brings to good is good.

Assumption: Death is a thing which brings to good.

Conclusion: Death is good.

Compound syllogisms are made up of two classes, the connexive, and the disjunctive. Each variety is made up of a compound Proposition followed by a simple Assumption and a simple Conclusion.

The Proposition of a *connexive syllogism* is an "if . . . then" construction. Its Assumption either affirms or denies one of the Proposition's two clauses; and its Conclusion then follows from the Proposition's other clause. There are two kinds of connexives, called the "first mode," and the "second mode." In the *first mode* the Assumption affirms the first clause of the hypothetical, and the Conclusion affirms the second:

Proposition: If he is in London, then he is in England.

Assumption: But he is in London.

Conclusion: Therefore he is in England.

In the *second mode* of the connexive syllogism, the Assumption denies the second clause of the Proposition, and the Conclusion must then deny the first:

Proposition: If he is in London, then he is in England.

Assumption: But he is not in England.

Conclusion: Therefore he is not in London.

Finally, compound syllogisms may also be *disjunctive syllogisms*. Here the Proposition's clauses are linked by the disjunctive "or," and the Assumption either affirms or denies one of the Proposition's two clauses, leaving the Conclusion to deny or affirm the other. Again there are two modes. In the *first mode*, the Assumption denies either of the Proposition's clauses and the Conclusion must affirm the other:

Proposition: It is either day or it is night.

Assumption: It is not day.

Conclusion: Therefore, it is night.

In the *second mode* of the disjunctive syllogism, the Assumption affirms one of the clauses, and the Conclusion is left to deny the other:

Proposition: It is either day or it is night.

Assumption: It is day.

Conclusion: Therefore, it is not night.

Though syllogism is important to humanist logics, it is neither its only nor even its chief concern. See Introduction, part 1.

Testimony: An argument taken from what someone — human or divine — has said. To argue "from Plato's testimony" is to cite Plato.

Unlike (*Comparison of unlikes*): A comparison of quality; dissimile. See Comparison.

Notes

1. Critical commentaries on the *Analysis* are few. J. P. Thorne, "A Ramistical Commentary on Sidney's 'Apologie for Poetrie,'" *MP* 54 (1957): 158–64, summarizes many of Temple's arguments; George W. Hallam, "Sidney's Supposed Ramism," in *Renaissance Papers, 1963* (Southeastern Renaissance Conference, 1963), pp. 11–20, uses Temple to argue against suggestions that Sidney was a "Ramist." Hallam comments on Temple without having read the *Analysis* except in Thorne's précis. Jan van Dorsten has also consulted the manuscript in order to establish the textual authority of its English phrases for his edition of the *Apology* in *Miscellaneous Prose of Sir Philip Sidney*, ed. Katherine Duncan-Jones and Jan van Dorsten (Oxford: Clarendon Press, 1973). Finally, my own article, "Oration and Method in Sidney's *Apology*: A Contemporary's Account," *MP* 79 (1981): 1–15, contrasts Temple's description of Sidney's organization with twentieth-century descriptions of the work as a seven-part oration.

2. *Gabriel Harvey's Ciceronianus*, intro. and notes by Harold S. Wilson, trans. by Clarence A. Forbes, University of Nebraska. Studies in the Humanities, no. 4 (Lincoln: University of Nebraska, 1945).

3. Other analyses in English are of Biblical texts. Temple himself wrote *A Logicall Analysis of Twentye Select Psalmes* (London, 1605). See also Dudley Fenner's analysis of the Lord's Prayer in *Certain godly and learned treatises* (Edinburgh, 1592), and Richard Sherry's translation of Johann Brenz, *A verye fruit-full exposicion vpon the syxte chapter of Saynte Iohn* (London, 1550). On the continent, a few analyses of more strictly literary works appeared. See, for example, Johannes Piscator, *M. T. Ciceronis De Officiis Librorum III Analysis Dialectica: ad praeceptiones P. Rami potissimum accommodata* (Spirae Nementum, 1596), and Petrus Ramus, *P. Virgilii Maronis Bucolica* (Paris, 1558).

4. See, for example, Rosemond Tuve, *Elizabethan and Metaphysical Imagery: Renaissance Poetic and Twentieth-Century Critics* (Chicago: University of Chicago Press, 1947).

5. The most interesting of these passages is Temple's paraphrase of Sidney's often-cited description of the poet's independence from nature: "Onely the Poet, disdayning to be tied to any such subiection, lifted vp with the vigor of his owne inuention, dooth growe in effect another nature . . ." (*An Apologie for*

Poetry, in G. Gregory Smith, ed., *Elizabethan Critical Essays*, [Oxford: Oxford University Press, 1904], 1:157). Much depends on this passage; since the term "inuention" seems to suggest a capacity of mind, Sidney's phrase suggests an image of the poet "lifted up with the vigor of his imagination" (see for example D. H. Craig's reading of the term in "A Hybrid Growth: Sidney's Theory of Poetry in *An Apology for Poetry*," *ELR* 10 [1980], esp. 184, 191–92). The problem in this, however, is that the idea of a poet-centered aesthetic, where the poet's special character is defined through an internally conceived capacity of mind, seems more of the nineteenth than of the sixteenth century. Temple's paraphrase, however, "in the polish of the work of art they produce" (*"in producti opificii expolitione"*) gives the passage a very different complexion. For Temple clearly understands "invention" not as a capacity of mind at all, but as the poem itself, "the thing invented." In Temple's version all foreshadowings of the Romantic poet disappear; it is not the poet's imagination but rather the thing the poet makes which lifts him to range in the zodiac of his wit. For similar examples of Temple's paraphrasings which are particularly suggestive, see Translation notes 25 and 44.

6. *Sir Philip Sidney as Literary Craftsman* (Cambridge, Mass.: Harvard University Press, 1935), pp. 46–83.

7. For discussion of Method see Walter J. Ong, *Ramus, Method, and the Decay of Dialogue* (Cambridge, Mass.: Harvard University Press, 1958), Neal W. Gilbert, *Renaissance Concepts of Method* (New York: Columbia University Press, 1960), and Lisa Jardine, *Francis Bacon: Discovery and the Art of Discourse* (Cambridge: Cambridge University Press, 1974), esp. pp. 1–65. See also William F. Edwards' "Niccolo Leoniceno and the Origins of Humanist Discussions of Method," in Edward P. Mahoney, ed., *Philosophy and Humanism: Renaissance Essays in Honor of Paul Oskar Kristeller* (New York: Columbia University Press, 1976), pp. 283–305. With respect to Sidney and Temple, see my "Oration and Method in Sidney's *Apology*." I also discuss Method below in this introduction.

8. See Translation note 3 for more information on Temple's use of the title *"de Poesi."*

9. The best explications of Tudor logic are Lisa Jardine's *Francis Bacon*, pp. 1–65; and her two articles, "Humanism and the Sixteenth Century Cambridge Arts Course," *History of Education* 4, no. 1: 16–31, and "The Place of Dialectic Teaching in Sixteenth-Century Cambridge," *Studies in the Renaissance* 21 (1974): 31–62. The best general survey of humanist logic is Wilhelm Risse, *Logik der Neuzeit* (Stuttgart-Bad Cannstatt: Friedrich Fromann, 1964), vol. 1. W. S. Howell, *Logic and Rhetoric in England: 1500–1700* (New York: Russell and Russell, 1961) is useful, but overemphasizes the differences between the different humanist logics.

10. Rudolph Agricola, *De Inventione dialectica* (Frankfurt/Main, 1967), p. 193; Philip Melanchthon, *Erotemata Dialectices* (1580), in Carolus Gottlieb Brettschneider, ed., *Corpus Reformatorum* (Halis Saxonum, 1846), 13:513; Ramus, see Temple's *P. Rami Dialecticae libri duo* (Cambridge, 1584), p. 1; Thomas Wilson, *The Rule of Reason conteyning the Arte of Logique*, ed. Richard S. Sprague (Northridge: San Fernando Valley State College, 1972), p. 8.

11. Abraham Fraunce, *Lawiers Logike* (London, 1588), p. 2a.

12. The sense that Ramus' logic is revolutionarily different from its

predecessors is argued by Tuve's *Elizabehan Imagery*. Her concomitant claim that Ramism explains Metaphysical poetry turned this subject into a modern battlefield. As Jardine's recent work shows (see note 9), the ground was ill-chosen, yet for some ten years after Tuve's book, scholars argued hard not only against Tuve's claims for the logical base of Metaphysical poetry, but also against Ramism. See for example Norman E. Nelson, "Peter Ramus and the Confusion of Logic, Rhetoric and Poetry," *University of Michigan Contributions in Modern Philology*, 2 (1947), pp. 1–22, and A. J. Smith, "An Examination of Some Claims for Ramism," *RES* n.s., 7, no. 28 (1956): 348–59. Howell's *Logic and Rhetoric* is less polemical, but he takes as fundamental the opposition between what he calls "traditional" or "Aristotelian" logic and Ramist logic. Neal Gilbert, *Renaissance Concepts of Method*, suggests a better way of understanding the relation between the two systems. He sees both as greatly simplified learning aids and suggests that Ramus' version seemed most shocking to other humanists because it showed the logical superficiality that all of them had been moving towards: "When Peter Ramus put out [his] even more elementary and perfunctory set of textbooks...some realization of the Pandora's box that had been opened began to dawn on startled scholars" (p. 73). But the point is that Ramism is not an aberration to humanism. If anything it shows only too clearly what educators from Valla onwards had been aiming at.

13. Jardine summarizes this debate in *Francis Bacon*, pp. 59–65.

14. Cited by S. A. Tannenbaum, "Some Unpublished Harvey Marginalia," *MLR* 25 (1930): 331.

15. *An Apologie for Poetrie*, in G. Gregory Smith, ed., *Elizabethan Critical Essays* (Oxford: Oxford University Press, 1904), 1:157. All further references to the *Apology* are to this text.

16. In Sister Mary Martin McCormick, ed., "A Critical Edition of Abraham Fraunce's 'The Sheapheardes Logike' and 'Twooe General Discourses,' " Dissertation, St. Louis University, 1968, p. 78. This very useful text is available through University Microfilms.

17. Temple, *P. Rami Dialecticae libri duo* (Cambridge, 1584), p. 63.

18. *Dialectique (1555), édition critique avec introduction, notes et commentaires de Michel Dassonville* (Geneva: Librairie Droz, 1964), p. 117. Because Ramus' French language edition is the most easily available version of his work, references to Ramus himself are to it.

19. See Jardine, *Francis Bacon*, p. 63: for Temple, *"methodus* is a term only to be used in the context of teaching and laying out material for clarity and comprehensiveness."

20. Traditional rhetoric had five parts: beyond Ramus' Elocution and Delivery, rhetoric included Invention, Disposition, and Memory. Ramus justified his simplification by pointing out that since both Invention and Disposition were treated by logic, to treat them in rhetoric as well was only to be redundant. And as for Memory, Ramus argued that this was only an adjunct to a proper use of Method: if one understood exactly how something was organized, then one had a perfect key to keeping it in memory. It is not so much in abbreviating rhetoric, then, that Ramus changes the art, since when used with the logic (as Ramus intended it to be), all the traditional parts were still there. But what is very different is that virtually all the formulas for traditional oratory, like the five or seven part oration, have been simplified to

Ramus' two Methods, the natural and the prudential. See Translation note 17 for more on the two Methods.

21. Abraham Fraunce, *The Arcadian Rhetorike*, ed. Ethel Seaton (Oxford: Luttrell Society, 1950), chap. 12, p. 26. Though this phrase is specifically used of Figures, it is appropriate to Tropes as well.

22. Pp. 85, 87. (I have changed Forbes' translation slightly. Where I translate "Both these," Forbes translates, "Both these methods of analysis," adding a non-technical and unnecessary sense of Method to his English rendition. Though Forbes' translation is generally superb, he does not always understand nuances of Ramist terminology.)

23. Murray Kreiger, *Theory of Criticism: A Tradition and Its System* (Baltimore and London: Johns Hopkins University Press, 1976), p. 76.

24. Among the Italian poets, both Mazzoni and Tasso wrote on this issue, each with his own interpretation of poetry's essential quality, but both also defining poetry as a logical art. Mazzoni's argument was that poetry's images were false, and thus that poetry was to be classed as a branch of sophistic logic, the logic of apparent truth. For him poetry's images do not imitate the true; rather they work to make the false seem believable. But even if poetry's fictions are false, they still depend for meaning upon rational processes and are therefore logical. Tasso, on the other hand, argues against Mazzoni that poetry's fictions are not at all false. Like Sidney, Tasso believes that poetry takes Ideas for its objects of imitation, and thus though poetry's images are feigned, they are not on that account false. But again, though the resulting "true" fictions have for Tasso a very different status than they have for Mazzoni, they are for him no less logical; instead of placing poetry under sophistic logic, Tasso classes it with dialectic, the logic of the probable. See Allan H. Gilbert, *Literary Criticism: Plato to Dryden* (New York: American Book Co., 1940), esp. pp. 367-70, 473-78. For a short summary of poetry-as-logic theories, see O. B. Hardison, Jr., *The Enduring Monument* (Chapel Hill: University of North Carolina Press, 1962), pp. 11-18.

25. See Jacob Bronowski, *The Poet's Defense* (Cambridge: Cambridge University Press, 1937), pp. 21-23. See also Arthur Kinney, *Markets of Bawdrie: The Dramatic Criticism of Stephen Gosson* (Salzburg: Institut für Englische Sprache, 1974), p. 48.

26. *The Schoolmaster (1570)*, ed. Lawrence V. Ryan (Charlottesville: University of Virginia Press, 1967), pp. 63-69.

27. In Kinney, p. 89.

28. *Oxford History of English Literature* (Oxford: The Clarendon Press, 1954), p. 346.

29. E. K.'s remark is in the Epistle to *The Shepheardes Calender*, in Ernest de Selincourt, ed., *Spenser's Minor Poems* (Oxford: The Clarendon Press, 1910), p. 6.

30. Part II of this introduction is a much extended version of a paper delivered at the Fourth International Congress for Neo-Latin Studies, Bologna, 1979.

31. See G. K. Hunter's excellent description of the Tudor scholar-courtier ideal in *John Lyly* (London: Routledge, Kegan and Paul; Cambridge, Mass.: Harvard University Press, 1962), pp. 1-35.

32. The Temple-Digby debate is well described by Lisa Jardine, *Francis Bacon*, pp. 59-65.

33. *Sir Philip Sidney: The Defense of Poesie, Political Discourses, Correspondences, Translations,* ed. Albert Feuillerat (Cambridge: Cambridge University Press, 1923), p. 145.

34. The *H M C* volume describes the manuscript as a quarto in 66 pp.; J. P. Thorne corrects this description, reporting that the manuscript is in fact an octavo, but he then adds, surprisingly, that the manuscript has 96 pages. The discepancies between the *H M C*'s 66 pp., Thorne's 96 pp., and the microfilm's 80 pp., however, are not as mysterious as they seem. Temple's *text* is indeed 66 pp., as the *H M C* describes it. And Thorne's brief account of the gathering's foliation suggests that his "96" is a misprint for "76." Since Thorne does not include in his page count the two folio leaves which comprise the cover-sheet/title page, when those four pages are added to the 76 pages his foliation suggests, the total of 80 pages agrees precisely with the microfilm.

William Temple's *Analysis* of Sir Philip Sidney's *Apology for Poetry*

Decastichon in Laudem
illustrissimi viri Phi-
lippi Sidnei Equitis
aurati.

Qui musas ornat removetque a crimine, nonne
  Ille mihi Musis annumerandus erit?
Ille mihi est natus Parnassi in collibus: illum
  Castaliae Phoebus flumine sparsit aquae.
Quid? non Sidneius nitidas Parnassidos umbrae
  A labe ad laudem vindicat arte Deas?
En vicit Stagyra[1] Platanique umbracula vicit
  Mantua Pierio nobilitata choro.
Ille ergo est natus Parnassi in collibus: illi
  Est Latonigenae laurea danda Dei.

Propos. ib. Qui musas.
Assump. ib. Quid? non.
Conclus. ib. ille ergo.

            Tuae dignitatis observantiss.
                Willm Temple.

A Ten-Verse Poem in Praise
of the Most Noble
Philip Sidney,
Knight

Whoever adorns the Muses and frees them from blame, should he not be numbered for me among the Muses? For me such a one was born on the peaks of Parnassus; Phoebus sprinkled him with the Castalian stream.

What then? Has not Sidney through his art brought from blame to praise the shining goddesses of the Parnassian shade? Look how Mantua, ennobled by the Pierian choir, conquered the Stagarite and the plane tree grove.[1]

Sidney therefore was born on the peaks of Parnassus; to him is due the laurel bough of the divine son of Latona.[2]

Proposition: Whoever praises the Muses.
Assumption: What then? Has not Sidney through his art?
Conclusion: Sidney therefore.

Most observant of your worthiness,
William Temple

Analysis tractationis de Poesi
contextae a nobilissimo viro
Philippe Sidneio equite
aurato.

Antequam aggrederis tractationem de Poesi (praestantissime Sidneie)
praefaris de causa susceptae defensionis & de venia tibi concedenda.
Adducor (inquis) ut poeseos defensionem aggrediar. Ad hujus enuntiati illustrationem attulisti efficientem causam. Quae igitur est
susceptae defensionis efficiens? certe philautia.
philautiam tuam similium comparatione declaras:
    ut Puglianum philautia impulit ad scientiam rei equestris
    ornandam.
Sic me philautia movit ad suscipiendam defensionem poeseos.
Protasis ibi: When the right vertuous.
Apodosis ibi: wherin yf Pugliano his.
    Protasis est longiuscula multiplicis argumenti complexa
    elegantiam.
    Primum est ab adjunctis auditoribus orationis a Pugliano habitae.
        Auditores e subjecto loco nempe Aula Caesaris & adjuncto
        studio rei equestris perdiscendae describuntur. |f. 6ᵛ|
        Secundum est ab adjuncto munere, quo Puglianus fungebatur
        in Aula Caesaris.
        Tertium ab adjuncta ubertate ingenii in Pugliano: quae ef-
        fectis suis exponitur, sed comparatione tractatis. Erudivit
        (inquis) nos non solum presenti demonstratione quantum
        facultate equestri excelleret, sed etiam ejus contemplatione
        multiplici.
Contemplationes istas equestris facultatis collatione Minorum ex-
plicatas habemus:
    Omnes Pugliani contemplationes obtundebant aures nostras.
    sed illa theoria quae in laudatione artificii equestris consumpta
    est, maxime.

An analysis of the treatise *On Poetry*[3]
written by the most noble
Philip Sidney,
knight

Before you begin your treatise *On Poetry* (most eminent Sidney) you
speak first about the cause for the defense you have undertaken, and
about an indulgence which is to be extended to you.

I am led (you say) to undertake the defense of poetry. To illustrate
this statement you have set forth an efficient cause; what is the efficient cause for the present defense? Surely it is "self-love" ["selfe-
loue is better then any guilding to make that seeme gorgious wherein
our selues are parties" (150)].

You declare your self-love through a comparison of likes:

As self-love brought Pugliano to embellish the science of
horsemanship,

So self-love moves me to undertake a defense of poetry.

Protasis: "When the right vertuous *Edward Wotton* and I were at the
Emperors Court together, wee gaue our selues to learne horsemanship of *Iohn Pietro Pugliano*, one that with great commendation had
the place of an Esquire in his stable" (150).

Apodosis: "Wherin, if *Pugliano* his strong affection and weake
arguments will not satisfie you, I wil giue a neerer example of my
selfe" (50).

The Protasis is rather long, its elegance made up of several
arguments.

The first argument is from the adjuncts of the listeners to
Pugliano's speech.

The listeners are described both from the subject of the
place — namely the Emperor's Court — and from the adjunct
of their eagerness to learn horsemanship well.

The second argument is from the adjunct of the office Pugliano
held in the Emperor's Court.

The third argument is from the adjunct of Pugliano's fertility of
wit, which is shown through its effects, treated in a comparison.

He taught us (you say) how much he excelled in horsemanship,
not only by actual demonstration, but also by various contemplations on the subject.

These contemplations on horsemanship are explained for us through
a comparison from the lesser:

All Pugliano's contemplations were striking to our ears;

But that theory which was devoted to praise of the master
horseman was most striking.

Comparationis hujus apodosis habet exornationem ab efficientibus
laudationis, nempe aliorum tarditate in dissolvendis stipendiis &
auditorum admiratione.

Porro Puglianicae laudationis theoria tractatur variis argumentis.
1. collatione Similium. ut milites nobilissimi hominum: sic equites
nobilissimi militum.
2. adjunctis: quod equites sint & principes in bello & ornamenta
pacis, in itinere celeres muniti ad locum occupandum victores
laureati & in acie & in aula.
3. effecto. facultas equestris principem ciuibus admirabilem red-
dit. sed effectum istud Minorum comparatione comprehenditur.
4. collatione Minorum. plena comparatio ejusmodi esset: Ars
regendae reipub. est exile & minutum quiddam: at facultas
equestris est longe praestantissima. |f. 7|
5. Subjecto facultatis equestris, nempe equo: quem Puglianus
laudavit e Minoribus & enumeratione adjunctorum.

Ad concludendam Pugliani laudationem equestris facultatis, tu tam
concinnae theoriae duo effecta notavisti, videlicet duplicem in te o-
pinionem ex illa natam: alteram de praestanti conditione equorum
(pene enim tibi de metamorphosi persuasisset) alteram de vi
philautiae ad rem ornandam & illuminandam. philautiae vis e
Minoribus arguitur.

Vides iam quomodo causam susceptae defensionis explicaveris. res tota
est enuntiati judicio tractata: quippe ita exposita sit hominum sen-
sibus & naturâ sua illustris, ut syllogismi lumen non desideret.

Veniae petitio concluditur syllogismo explicato secundae speciei.
argumentum est a genere.
Quicunque discipulus magistri vestigia sequitur, ei erranti ignosci
debetur.
Ego magistri vestigia sequor.
[Mihi] itaque ignosci debet[ur].
Propos. ib. since the scholler.

The second term of this comparison is embellished from the efficient causes of the praise, namely from other students' slow payment of their bills, and from the listeners' admiration ["either angred with slowe paiment, or mooued with our learner-like admiration" (150)]. Next the theory of Pugliano's praise is dealt with through various arguments:

1. by a comparison of likes: as soldiers are the noblest of men, so horsemen are the noblest of soldiers.
2. through adjuncts: because horsemen are masters of war and ornaments of peace, swift in going, strong in holding a place, decorated victors in both the battle-field and the court.
3. through effect: horsemanship makes a prince admirable to the people. This effect is also dealt with through a comparison:
4. through a comparison from the lesser: the full comparison would be like this: the art of government is somehow thin and meager, but the skill of horsemanship is most excellent by far.
5. through the subject of horsemanship, namely the horse, which Pugliano praised by a comparison from the lesser, and through an enumeration of adjuncts.

To conclude Pugliano's praise of the equestrian faculty, you have noted two effects of his so elegantly polished theory, i.e., two opinions you now hold that have arisen from it: the first of these concerns the peerless character of horses (such that he might almost have persuaded you to be transformed into a horse yourself); the second concerns the force that self-love has for adorning and embellishing something. This force of self-love is argued from a comparison from the lesser ["selfe-loue is better than any guilding to make that seeme gorgious wherein our selues are parties" (150)].

You now see how you have laid out the cause of this defense; the whole thing has been treated by the disposition of axiom. For surely it should be so well set forth to men's senses, so clear in its essential nature, that your exposition should have no need of the light of syllogism.[4]

You include your request for indulgence in a full syllogism of the second figure. The argument is from genus:

Any disciple who follows the footsteps of a master is to be pardoned when he errs.

I follow the footsteps of a master.

Therefore, I am to be pardoned.

Proposition: "sith the scholler is to be pardoned that foloweth the steppes of his Maister" (151).

Assumptio deest.

Conclus. ib. Beare wth me.

Sed omissae Assumptionis loco illustrationem assumptionis subjecisti
  ab effecto comparato: quod scilicet rem major studio quam argumento tractes: id quod Pugliano contigit. Deinde hoc ipsum effectum,
  in quo te magistri imitatorem praestas, adhibita correctione exor-
  nas: Ais enim opus esse, ut |f. 7^v| illustriorem quam ille & ner-
  vosiorem probationem afferas ad defensionem poetarum.

Necessitatem magis nervosae probationis urges e similibus:
  Protas. ib. And yet J must.
  Apodo. ib. So have J need.

Protasin arguis ab efficiente defensionis suscipiendae, nempe poeseos
  contemptu in hominibus.

Apodosis etiam arguitur ab efficiente nervosioris probationis. efficiens
  ista concluditur enthymemate.
  Jn poesin philosophi calumniam contulerunt.
  Ad poeseos igitur defensionem nervosior demonstratio adhibenda est.

Anteced. ib. The silly later. enthymematis antecedens illustratur
  dissimili:
  Superior illa facultas nunquam privata est debita laude.
  At poesin philosophi calumniati sunt.

Hactenus praefatus es: sequitur jam ipsa tractatio de poesi.

Tua De Poesi tractatio sita est partim in confirmatione veritatis, partim
  in refutatione calumniae.

Veritatis confirmatio ad amplificandam laudem poeseos multis
  argumentis disputatur.

Primum est ab adjuncto. concluditur syllogismo explicato secundae
  speciei. |f. 8|
    Antiquissimam disciplinam & caeterarum disciplinarum parentem
      calumniantes philosophi non possunt effugere crimen ingrati
      animi.
    Poesis est antiquissima disciplina & caeterarum disciplinarum
      parens.

Assumption: omitted.

Conclusion: "beare with me" (151).

In place of the omitted Assumption you have inserted an illustration of it from a comparison of effect: like Pugliano, you would evidently treat the matter more through good will than through reason. Then you embellish this same effect—in which you excell yourself as an imitator of the master—by suggesting a correction: for you say that it is necessary that you should produce a more clear and vigorous argument for the defense of poets than Pugliano produced for horsemanship.

You urge the need for a stronger proof from a comparison of likes:

> Protasis: "And yet I must say that as I haue iust cause to make a pittiful defence of poore Poetry" (151).
>
> Apodosis: "so haue I need to bring some more auaileable proofes" (151).

You argue the Protasis of this comparison from the efficient cause of the defense you have undertaken, namely from men's contempt for poetry.

The Apodosis is then argued from the efficient cause of this stronger proof. That efficient cause is given in an enthymeme:

> Philosophers have brought calumny to poetry.
>
> Therefore a stronger argument should be used to defend poetry.

Antecedent:[5] "the silly latter hath had euen the names of Philosophers vsed to the defacing of it" (151). This Antecedent is illustrated by unlikeness:

> That faculty discussed earlier [i.e., horsemanship] has never been deprived of its proper praise.
>
> But philosophers have slandered poetry.

So far, all you have said has been preface. Now follows the treatise itself on poetry.

Your treatise On Poetry consists partly in a confirmation of the true nature of poetry, partly in a refutation of calumny.

To amplify the praise of poetry, the confirmation of truth is set out through several arguments.

The first argument is from adjunct. It is concluded in a full syllogism of the second figure:

> In slandering the most ancient discipline and parent of all other disciplines, philosophers cannot escape the charge of ungratefulness.
>
> Poetry is the oldest discipline and the parent of all other disciplines.

Poesin itaque calumniantes philosophi non possunt effugere crimen
    ingrati animi.
Propos. ib. And first truly. illustratur duplici collatione similium: altera
    ab histrice, altera a vipera.
Assumptio partim ib. Who having been the first. partim ib. For not
    only.
Assumptionis pars prima de antiquitate confirmatur inductione
    specialium:
        Poesis Musaei, Homeri, Hesiodi, Orphei, Lini est omnibus
        disciplinis antiquior.
        Poesis igitur est antiquissima disciplina.

Probari doctissimis viris antecedentem enthymematis non ignoro. Ego
    tamen mathematicae artis disciplinam, quam antiquissimi fere
    Hebraei quibusdam columnis incîderunt, poesi istorum hominum
    antiquiorem esse puto: nisi fortasse Noae temporibus floruerint.

Assumptionis pars secunda de caeterarum artium procreatione
    demonstratur effecto poeseos: quod scilicet agrestes hominum animos
    ad doctrinae admirationem rapuerit instrumento divinae cujusdam
    suavitatis.
        Subjicitur probatio hujus effecti e speciebus:
            Poesis Amphionis & Orphei, Livii, & Ennii, Dantis & Pe-
            trarchae, Goweri & Chawceri rapuit hominum animos ad
            doctrinae admirationem.
            Poesis itaque id praestat. |f. 8ᵛ|

Atqui vero (nobilissime Sidneie) isto argumento effect[i] non efficitur
    poesin esse caeterarum artium parentem. N[am] admiratio doc-
    trinae, quam poesis parit, significat doctrinam jam natam esse. Quî
    enim potest esse admiratio rei, quae nondum in natura extiterit?
    Fateor admiratione excitatos esse homines ad studium doctrinae jam
    natae. Atque id fortasse est quo[d] vi poeticae facultatis efficitur.
    Quaeritur vero non utrum poesis homines excitaverit ad studium

In slandering poetry, therefore, philosophers cannot escape the charge of ungratefulness.

Proposition:[6] "And first, truly to al them that professing learning inueigh against Poetry, may iustly be obiected, that they goe very neer to vngratfulnes" (151). This is illustrated by a double comparison of likes, the first to a hedgehog, the second to a viper.

Assumption: partly "who, hauing beene the first of that Country that made pens deliuerers of their knowledge to their posterity, may iustly chalenge to bee called their Fathers in learning" (151), and partly "for not only in time they had this priority (although in it self antiquity be venerable) but went before them, as causes to drawe with their charming sweetnes the wild vntamed wits to an admiration of knowledge" (151).

The first part of this Assumption, dealing with antiquity, is confirmed by an induction of specials:

The poetry of Musaeus, Homer, Hesiod, Orpheus, Linus, is older than all disciplines.

Poetry, therefore, is the oldest discipline.

I know that the first term of this last enthymeme has been argued by very learned men. Nevertheless, I believe that the discipline of mathematics, which the well-nigh most ancient Hebrews inscribed in certain columns, is older than the poetry of these men; unless perhaps poets flourished in the times of Noah.[7]

You demonstrate the Assumption's second part, concerning the origin of the other arts, from the effect of poetry, that surely poetry, by means of a certain divine sweetness, drew the wild wits of men to an admiration of knowledge.

The proof of this effect is taken from species:[8]

The poetry of Amphion and Orpheus, Livy and Ennius, Dante and Petrarch, Gower and Chaucer, drew men's wits to an admiration of knowledge.

Poetry, therefore, is responsible for this.

And yet truly (most noble Sidney) this argument of yours from effect does not make poetry the parent of the other arts. For the admiration of knowledge to which poetry gives birth indicates that learning had already been created. For how can there be an admiration of something that does not yet exist in nature? I grant that men have been moved by admiration to the study of knowledge that already exists, and perhaps it is that which is brought about by the power of the poetic faculty. But the question is really not whether poetry should have moved men to study a discipline that had already been

disciplinae jam observatae, sed utrum poeseos beneficio disciplinae primum inventae sint. illud potest ab admiratione proficisci: hoc alterius causae est.

Ut argumento speciei probatum est hominum animos rapi a poesi ad doctrinae admirationem: sic idem probare vis ab adjuncto: est enim poeseos adjunctum ut adhibeatur a philosophis & historicis. res est conclusa enthymemate:

> Philosophi & historici usi sunt apparatu poetico cum se populo dare & publicam lucem aspicere voluerunt.
>
> Poesis itaque rapit hominum animos ad admirationem doctrinae.

Anteced. ib. This did so notablely. & ib. And even Historiographers. repetitur ib. So that truly nether.

Antecedens tractatur inductione specialium. ib. So Thales, Empedocles and Parmenides. ubi argumento effectorum Solo et Plato transferuntur in numerum poetarum. inductionis pars de Historicis ib. So Herodotus. ubi ex effectis doces historicos fuisse poetas. |f. 9|

Secundum argumentum de laude poeseos est ab adjuncta communitate: ut primum erat ab adjuncta antiquitate:

> Poesis sic est fusa communiter ut a Barbaris nationibus colatur, id est, Turcis, Hibernis, Indis, Wallis.
>
> Quis igitur de laude poeseos dubitabit?

Anteced. ib. in all wch they have.

De enthymematis consecutione vereor ut tibi possim concedere. si illud verum sit rem minime bonam coli & probari posse communiter a Barbaris nationibus: ut perversam de Deo opinionem. At hujusmodi opinio non ideo laudanda est.

established, but whether disciplines were first invented as a result
of poetry. The study of a discipline that has already been established
can proceed from admiration; but the invention of such disciplines
has another cause.[9]

Just as it is demonstrated by an argument from species that poetry
draws men's wits to an admiration of knowledge, so you also want
to prove the same thing from the adjunct; for it is an adjunct of poetry
that it should be used by philosophers and by historians. The matter is set out in an enthymeme:

> Philosophers and historians have used the devices of poetry when
> they wanted to appear to the world and to face popular
> judgment.

Therefore poetry draws men's wits to an admiration of knowledge.
Antecedent:[10] "This did so notably shewe it selfe, that the Phylosophers
of Greece durst not a long time appeare to the worlde but vnder
the masks of Poets" (152). And: "And euen Historiographers
(although theyr lippes sounde of things doone, and veritie be written in theyr fore-heads) haue been glad to borrow both fashion and
perchance weight of Poets" (152–53). It is repeated at "So that, truly, neyther Phylosopher nor Historiographer coulde at the first haue
entred into the gates of populer iudgements, if they had not taken
a great pasport of Poetry" (153).

The Antecedent is dealt with through an induction of specials: "So
Thales, Empedocles, and *Parmenides* sange their naturall Phylosophie
in verses" (152), where by an argument of effects Solon and Plato
are moved into the ranks of the poets. Part of the induction concerns historians: "So *Herodotus* entituled his Historie by the name
of the nine Muses" (153), where from effects you explain that
historians were poets.

The second argument in praise of poetry is from the adjunct of community, just as the first was from the adjunct of antiquity:

> Poetry is so widely diffused that it is even cultivated by barbarous
> nations, i.e., The Turks, the Irish, the Indians, the Welsh.
> So who will doubt the praise of poetry?

Antecedent:[11] "in all which they haue some feeling of Poetry" (153).
With respect to the logical force of your enthymeme, I fear I should
not allow it to you. Even if it should be true that barbarous nations
can all jointly cultivate and recommend a view that is the least bit
good, in the same way that they all jointly hold a perverse idea of
God, still an idea of this sort should not be praised on this account
alone.[12]

Ex Indorum effecto colligis fore poesin siquid aliud, procreatricem apud Indos philosophiae.

Poeticae facultatis studium apud Wallos illustras Diversis:
Etsi Wallorum hostes omnibus Wallorum disciplinis interitum parabant: tamen poesis remansit ad hunc usque diem: id quod *parium collatione* exornas. ib. So as it is not.
Tertium argumentum est ab adjunctis poetarum nominibus.
Poeta appellatur Vates & ποιητής.
Laudandus[2] igitur.
Anteced. partim ib. Among the Romanes. partim ib. the Greekes called hym. ubi est antecedentis declaratio e nominis efficientibus.
|f. 9ᵛ| Antecedentis pars prima de Vate arguitur notatione nominis.
Poetica facultate significatio rei futurae judicata est contineri.
Poeta igitur recte appellatur Vates.

Illa nominis notatio Romanorum Caesarum & nominatim Albini effecto confirmatur: ut qui sese in sortibus Virgilianis, consueverint exercere.
Romanorum Caesarum effectum cum argumento Diversorum tum effecto Apollinis & Sybillae defenditur. Nam uterque oracula versibus tradidit. Hîc effecti Apollinei & Sybillini efficientem notas nempe in numero & afflatu poetico divinam quandam vim. Huc etiam Davidis effectum additur ad Romanorum Caesarum defendendam actionem. David enim sua opera versibus complexus est.

Davidem opera sua versibus complexum esse doces primum e testimonio veterum & novorum scriptorum: partim ib. yf J doe it J shall not.[3] partim ib. it is fully written in meeter.
Deinde ab adjuncto nomine, quod appellentur psalmi.
tum ab adjuncta ratione tractationis, quae prorsus est poetica.

From an argument of effect on Indians, you conclude that if anything, poetry will be the mother of philosophy among the Indians ["if euer learning come among them, it must be by hauing theyr hard dull wits softned and sharpened with the sweete delights of Poetrie" (153)].

You illustrate the affection for poetry among the Welsh from the place of differences:

> Even though the enemies of the Welsh repeatedly set about to ruin all the learning of the Welsh, nevertheless poetry has endured even to this day. You embellish this by a comparison of equals: "so as it is not more notable in soone beginning then in long continuing" (153).

The third argument is from the adjunct of poets' names.

The poet is called *vates* and "poet."

He is therefore to be praised.

The Antecedent is partly: "Among the Romans a Poet was called *Vates*" (154), and partly: "The Greekes called him a Poet" (155), where the statement of the Antecedent is from the efficient causes of the name.[13]

The first part of the Antecedent, of *vates,* is argued from the word's etymology:

> The meaning of future events was thought to be held by poetry.
> The poet is therefore rightly called *vates.*

This etymology is confirmed through the effect of poetry on the Roman Emperors, and in particular, on Albinus, as men who were accustomed to practising *Sortes Virgilianae* — Virgilian prophecies.

> The effect of poetry on Roman Emperors is supported not only with an argument from difference, but also from the effect of Apollo and the Sybils. For each of these delivered oracles in verse. Here you note the efficient cause of the effect of Apollo and the Sybils, namely a certain divine force in versification and poetic inspiration. Then to defend what the Roman Emperors did, you add an argument from the effect of David, for David wrote his works in verse.[14]

That David wrote his works in verse you show first from the testimony of both ancient and modern learned men: "If I doo, I shall not do it without the testimonie of great learned men, both auncient and moderne" (154), and: "it is fully written in meeter, as all learned Hebricians agree" (155).

> Then you explain from the adjunct of name, as his poems are called "psalms."
> Then from the adjunct of the order of his handling, which is clearly poetic ["Lastly and principally, his handeling his prohecy, which is meerly poetical (155)].

Rationem tractationis illustras argumento formae. Nam
musici instrumenti experrectio, personarum crebra mutatio,
insignes prosopopeiae notant ipsam formam tractationis.
Davidis effectum concludis deprecatione prophanati nominis. Con-
tumeliam nomini Davidis illatam deprecaris argumento finis & ef-
fecti. ib. But they that wth quiett. |f. 10|
Antecedentis pars secunda περὶ ποιητοῦ habet exornationem ab adjuncto
illius generali usu: quia poetae nomen est in omnibus fere idiomatis
usurpatum.
   tum a notatione: ποιητής dicitur ἀπὸ τοῦ ποιεῖν: quam notationem
   ab effecto esse constat.
Graecorum effectum in nomine ποιητοῦ Poetis tribuendo comparatione
tractatur, nempe Simili effecto Anglorum. Atque hîc poetici nominis
dignitatem exaggeras e Comparatione Dissimilium:
Caeterae artes habent subjectas sibi naturae actiones & facultates, adeo
ut quas res natura exponi hominum oculis & repraesentari vult,
earum illae velut actores sint. ib. There is no art.
At poesis non est alligata naturae, sed velut altera natura aut rem jam
factam meliorem efficit quam effici potuit a natura aut fingit for-
matque tale quiddam quale nunquam in natura viguit. ib. Only the
poet.

Protasis confirmatur inductione specialium. ib. So doth the Astronomer
&&.

You illustrate the order of this handling by an argument of
form: the awakening of musical instruments, the frequent
changings of persons, the notable prosopopeias, all show that
same form of the handling.

You finish your treatment of David's effect with a plea for indulgence
should his name have been profaned ["But truely nowe hauing named
him, I feare mee I seeme to prophane that holy name, applying it
to Poetrie, which is among vs throwne downe to so ridiculous an
estimation" (155)]. You ask indulgence from any insult brought to
David's name with an argument of final cause and of effect: "but
they that with quiet iudgements will looke a little deeper into it, shall
finde the end and working of it such, as beeing rightly applyed,
deserueth not to bee scourged out of the Church of God" (155).

The second part of the Antecedent, of "poet," is embellished from the
adjunct of the general use of this term, for the name of "poet" has
been used in almost all languages.

The "poet" is embellished from etymology: "Poet," or "maker,"
derives from *poiein*, "to make." This etymology is clearly from
effect. [15]

The effect on the Greeks — that they gave the name *poeta* to poets — is
dealt with through a comparison, namely, through a similar effect
among the English. And here you elaborate upon the dignity of the
name of poetry in a comparison of unlikes:

[Protasis:] Other arts have as their subjects the actions and faculties
of nature; in so far as nature wishes these things to be set forth and
shown to men's eyes, these arts are, as it were, the actors of those
things: "There is no Arte deliuered to mankinde that hath not the
workes of Nature for his principall obiect, without which they could
not consist, and on which they so depend, as they become Actors
and Players, as it were, of what Nature will haue set foorth" (155).

[Adodosis:] But poetry is not bound to nature; rather, as if it were
another nature, it either brings forth an existing thing made better
than it could be made by nature, or it shapes and forms such things
as never flourished in nature: "Onely the Poet, disdayning to be tied
to any such subiection, lifted vp with the vigor of his owne inuention, dooth growe in effect another nature, in making things either
better then Nature bringeth forth, or, quite a newe, formes such
as neuer were in Nature as the *Heroes, Demigods, Cyclops, Chimeras,
Furies*, and such like" (156).

The Protasis is confirmed by an induction of specials: "So doth the
Astronomer looke vpon the starres, and, by that he seeth, setteth
downe what order Nature hath taken therein . . ." (155-56).

specialium inductio peccat & falsitate quarundam partium et
methodo. Ais spectari a rhetorica rationem persuadendi: at illa
tropos, figuras, pronuntiationem solummodo intuetur: adeo ut
finem suum assecuta sit si bene dicatur. dicere ad persuadendum hominis est non artis. Neque si aliqua vis sit in elocutione
& actione ad persuadendum, idcirco praeceptum de eo rhetorica
tradet. Logicae artis praeceptio valet ad numerationem: non
tamen logicae artis erit de numeratione praecipere. Quid quod
ne dialectica quidem de persuadendo praecipiat? subjectum
dialecticae erit toti arti commune. at persuasio non est totius
dialecticae. Nam cum persuasio viribus integrae sententiae
|f. 10ᵛ| efficiatur, inventio autem non integras sententias sed
integrae sententiae partes ab omni dispositione sejunctas consideret: non erit persuasio res ea quam logica inventio suis
praeceptis interpretatur. Ac cum finis logicae disciplinae non
in fortuito eventu positus sit sed intra artis potestatem semper
contineatur, persuasio autem e logicarum praeceptionum usu
non semper oriatur: qui fieri potest ut persuasio logicae
disciplinae finis sit? Metaphysica tibi abstractis notionibus con-
tinetur: atque [eo] nomine supernaturalem appellari putas: ver-
sari tamen in contemplatione naturae, sic ut quod in ea maxime reconditum est & retrusum, id intueatur & consideret. Affers (praestantissime Sidneie) metaphysicae a physiologia non
satis aptam differentiam. Nam physiologia tota est in abstractis notionibus: id est, res illas quas tractat, adhibita generali con-
sideratione generalibus theorematis comprehendit: immo
quaelibet fere ars subjectam materiam, quam praeceptis com-
plecti vult[,] abstractam mente & cognitione a singularibus in

This induction of specials errs both in the falsity of certain parts, and in method. You say that rhetoric considers the means of persuasion [i.e., "the Rethorician and Logitian, considering what in Nature will soonest proue and perswade, thereon giue artificial rules, which still are compassed within the circle of a question, according to the proposed matter" (156)], but rhetoric considers only tropes, figures, and delivery, so that it has achieved its proper purpose as long as it is spoken well.[16] Speaking in order to persuade has to do with the man, not with the art. Nor even if there should be some force for persuasion in elocution and rhetorical gesture will rhetoric for that reason deal with persuasion's precepts. The teachings of logic help one to count, but it still will not be logic's task to teach counting.

But how is it then that not even logic should teach persuasion? The subject of logic will be a property common to the whole art, but persuasion is not something to be found in all of logic. For while persuasion may be brought about by the force of sound thought, logical invention does not consider sound thoughts, but rather the parts of a sound thought, divorced from all considerations of disposition. Persuasion will not be what logical invention explains through its precepts. And since logic's purpose is not defined by something that arises only fortuitously, but is always circumscribed within the general power of the art, and since persuasion, for its part, does not always result from the use of logical precepts, how then could persuasion be a goal of logic?[17]

Metaphysics for you is made up of abstract notions, and from its name, you suppose both that the "supernatural" is spoken of and that metaphysics is concerned with the contemplation of nature in such a way that it may observe and consider that which is in nature especially hidden and deep [i.e., "And the Metaphisick, though it be in the seconde and abstract notions, and therefore be counted supernaturall, yet doth hee indeede builde vpon the depth of Nature" (156)]. But you do not make (most eminent Sidney) a sufficiently precise distinction between metaphysics and natural philosophy. For natural philosophy is entirely made up of abstract notions: that is, those things it treats, having brought a general consideration to bear upon them, it understands through the universals of theory. In fact, almost any art considers its subject matter—that which it wants to treat through its precepts—abstracted from singulars to the universal by means of the mind and the understanding. And

genere[4] contemplatur. Ac proinde abstractione ista, id est, rerum generali consideratione non efficitur ut metaphysica aut differat a physiologia aut supra naturam efferri dicatur. At ne contemplatio rei in natura maxime abstrusae valet ad metaphysicae a physiologia differentiam. potestne quid esse in natura magis abditum & occultum quam materia formaque rerum? quam ortae e forma proprietates? At physiologia materiam formasque rerum & e formis natas proprietates disquirit & praeceptis exponit suis. Convenit igitur metaphysicae cum physica. Quod si Aristotelicae metaphysicae sapientiam intelligimus, est illa quidem non una & singularis ars sed velut chaos quoddam e multarum artium concretum disciplinis, iisque non optimis & selectissimis sed jejunum |f. 11| sophisma & inanem subtilitatem complexis. Peccat igitur rerum falsitate specialium inductio. Ac cum Astronomiam & Musicam a corpore physiologiae sejungat, non est legi καθάυτό obsecuta. Nam si physiologiae omnia membra largiri volumus, debemus eidem contemplationem naturae in astris & sonis concedere.

De specialium methodo non est necesse pluribus disserere. Constat enim grammaticam rhetoricae, rhetoricam dialecticae, dialecticam arithmeticae, arithmeticam geometriae, geometriam physiologiae, physiologiam medicinae, medicinam jurisprudentiae, praeponendam esse. Attamen methodi κρύψιν illam, quae adhibetur, non improbo. est enim frequens in communi usu disserendi.

Antapodosis dissimilitudinis constat duabus partibus: quarum prior est de natura victa illa quidem a poetis, in producti opificii expolitione: posterior de efformatione rei quae nunquam extitit. Hanc posteriorem exemplis specialibus approbas contracto syllogismo conclusis. syllogismus integer sic est:

Heroes, semidei, Cyclopes, Chymerae nunquam extiterunt.

Heroes, semidei, Cyclopes, Chymerae efformantur a poetis.

Ac proinde res aliquae efformantur a poetis quae nunquam extiterunt.

therefore, this "abstract"-ness of yours, that is, this general consideration of things, does not result either in metaphysics' differing from natural philosophy, or in its being said to be raised above the natural. Thus it is not the studying of something that is most abstruse in nature that can serve as the difference between metaphysics and natural philosophy. Can anything in nature be more hidden and secret than matter and the form of things? than the properties which are derived from a form? Yet natural philosophy investigates matter and the forms of things, and the properties derived from forms, and it explains them through its precepts.[18] Thus metaphysics and natural philosophy meet. But then if we understand the wisdom of Aristotle's metaphysics, it is certainly not a single and a singular art anyway, but rather it is like a sort of chaos, made up from the disciplines of many arts, and not from those that are the best or most select, but rather from those that comprise a feeble sophism and empty subtlety.[19] Thus your induction from specials fails through the falsity of these things. And when it separates astronomy and music from the main body of natural philosophy, it fails to respect the integrity of natural philosophy's subject matter.[20] For if we want to give to natural philosophy all its proper members, we ought to give to that same field the study of nature in the case of stars and sounds.

Concerning the method with which you order these specials, it is not necessary to discuss this much. For it is well-known that grammar is to be put before rhetoric, rhetoric before dialectic, dialectic before arithmetic, arithmetic before geometry, geometry before natural philosophy, natural philosophy before medicine, medicine before law. Nevertheless, I do not object to the crypsis of method you use here, for it is frequently used in common organizational practice.[21]

The Antapodosis of the earlier unlikeness [i.e., that poetry, in not being bound to nature, is unlike any other art] consists of two parts: the first of these concerns nature's having in fact been surpassed by poets in the polish of the work of art they produce;[22] the second concerns making something that never existed. You argue this last part through special examples set out in a contracted syllogism. The whole syllogism is like this:

Heroes, Demi-gods, Cyclops, Chymeras never existed.
Heroes, Demi-gods, Cyclops, Chymeras are made by poets.
And therefore some things that have never existed are made by poets.

Comprehensum Assumptione errorem mox demonstrabo, cum illud
docebo fictionem istam non effici vi poeticae facultatis.

Prior antapodoseos pars amplificatur varia comparatione e Minoribus:
Poeta fabricam terrae ornatiorem reddidit quam natura.
Natura aeneum, poeta aureum mundum effinxit.
Natura amatorem, ducem belli, principem eleganter expressit: sed
poeta multo elegantius. |f. 11ᵛ|

Hoc loco ad refutandam prolepsin digrederis. Objici enim potest
naturae opus reipsa existere: opus vero poetae figmento cogitationis:
ideoque naturam a poeta non vinci dignitate. refellitur prolepsis dum
subjectum illud notas, in quo praestantia artificis & dignitas posita
est. Posita est (inquis) in idea operis non in ipso opere. Quid quod
ipsam ideae explicationem doceas non esse omnibus partibus
fictitiam?[5]

Primum adhibetur dissimilitudo ad ideae explicationem
distinguendam. Ideae explicatio non est eo modo fictitia ut ar-
cis in aere constructio.

Deinde attexitur comparatio Majorum, qua explicatur qualis sit
illa fictio:
Poesis non solum in specie praestantem effigiem exprimit sed
etiam in genere. ib. it worketh not only to make a Cyrus.

Naturae & poeseos collationem objectionis refutatione concludis.ib.
Nether let it bee deemed. Objectio e Diversis diluitur:
Non decet eum audaciae coarguere qui ejusmodi comparationem
instituit, sed Deo honorem ⌈deferre⌉ qui hanc facultatem poesi
concessit. Deum laudas ab effecto. Dei effectum collatione
Minorum arguitur:
Hominis illa divina vis ingenii aliis in rebus multum elucet:
at in poetica plurimum. sic enim Minorum comparatio,
quam tu contractam effecisti, suis partibus est distinguen-

I shall shortly show the basic error in the Assumption here, when I explain that this sort of fiction is not created through the force of the poetic faculty.[23]

And as for the first part of the Antapodosis, it is amplified by a varied comparison from the lesser:

The poet has delivered a more ornate feigning of the world than nature has.

Nature has fashioned a brass, the poet a golden world.

Nature has very elegantly given form to the lover, the leader in war, the prince, but the poet has done so much more elegantly.

At this point you turn to refuting a possible objection. For it can be objected that a work of nature exists in fact, while the work of the poet exists only in the image of a thought, and that for that reason, nature is not surpassed in worth by the poet. You refute this objection when you identify the subject in which the artist's preeminence and worth inhere. They inhere (you say) in the idea of the work, and not in the work itself. But how would you show that this delivering forth of an idea is not fictional in every part?[24]

First you suggest an unlikeness in order to clarify the delivering forth of an idea: the delivering forth of an idea is not fictional in the same way as is the building of a castle in the air.

Then you add a comparison from the greater to explain what sort of thing this fiction is.

Poetry not only expresses an outstanding image as a particular, but also as a universal: "it worketh, not onely to make a *Cyrus*, which had been but a particuler excellencie, as Nature might haue done, but to bestow a *Cyrus* vpon the worlde, to make many *Cyrus's*, if they wil learne aright why and how that Maker made him" (157).

You conclude the comparison of Nature and poetry by refuting an objection: "Neyther let it be deemed too sawcie a comparison to ballance the highest poynt of mans wit with the efficacie of Nature" (157). The objection is answered through an argument from differences:

It is not right to accuse anyone of impudence who makes such a comparison. Rather one should give the honor to God, who granted this power to poetry. You praise God from effect. The effect of God is argued in a comparison from the lesser:

That divine force of man's wit shines much in other things, but most of all in poetry. For this is how the comparison from the lesser, which you have put into a contracted form,

da[.] comparationis redditionem effecto declaras sed comparato cum Minore effecto naturae. ib. When wth the force of a divine breath. ubi effecti hujus efficiens notatur, nempe divinus afflatus. Hinc e divino afflatu ingenii & depravat[a] voluntate, id est, duobus hominum adjunctis argumentum colligis primi lapsus. |f. 12|

ADhuc Poesin ornasti ab adjuncto triplici, nimirum ab antiquitate, communitate, nominibus. Sequitur poeticae facultatis laus primum e definitione, tum e Distributione.

Poesis est ars imitationis seu fictionis ad Docendum & delectandum. Haec est illa definitio (illustrissime Philippe) quae totam controversiam continet: & qua tanquam fundamento instituta a te de Poesi tractatio fere nititur. Videamus igitur rectene rei definitae naturam explicet & definiat. Vis tu poeseos naturam fictione quadam comprehendi. Ecquid fictio ista aliud est quam inventio rei quae nondum extitit? Qui fingit, is logica argumenta fingit, nempe causas, effecta, subjecta, adjuncta, dissentanea, comparata aut caetera quae ex istis oriuntur. Sic Ovidius fingens regiam Solis finxit efficientem causam a qua constructa ⌈est⌉, materiam ex qua conflata est, adjuncta quibus ornata est. At fingere Causas, effecta, subjecta, adjuncta, caeteraque argumenta, nihil aliud est quam invenire causas, effecta, subjecta, adjuncta. Quamobrem fictio erit idem quod rei, quae nondum extiterit, inventio. id si ita est, ars fictionis non ad poesin sed ad dialecticam inventionem pertinebit: qua non solum res verae sed etiam fictitiae cogitantur. Fateor res ipsas quae finguntur, esse alterius disciplinae, ethicae quidem plerunque aut physicae, non minus quam argumenta illa quae in rerum natura cernuntur et vigent. At ipsa fictio perinde ac excogitatio horum argumentorum est actio nativae vel artificiosae rationis in inveniendo. Dum igitur

is to be divided into its parts. You state the second clause of this comparison through God's effect, but compared to the lesser effect of nature: "when with the force of a diuine breath he bringeth things forth far surpassing her dooings" (157). Here the efficient cause of this effect is noted, namely a divine breath. Then from this divine breath of wit and from the infected will, i.e., from two of mankind's adjuncts, you make an argument concerning the fall of man ["with no small argument to the incredulous of that first accursed fall of *Adam*: sith our erected wit maketh vs know what perfection is, and yet our infected will keepeth vs from reaching vnto it" (157)].

So far, you have described poetry by three adjuncts, namely, antiquity, community, and names. Next comes praise of the poetic faculty first from definition, then from distribution.

Poetry is an art of imitation, or of fiction-making (*fictio*), with the end of teaching and delighting.

This is the definition (most worthy Sidney) that holds the whole controversy, and on which, like a foundation, this treatise *On Poetry* that you teach almost entirely stands. Let us see, then, whether it explains and defines rightly the nature of the thing you have defined.[25]

You want the essential nature of poetry to be understood as a certain kind of fiction-making. But can it be that such a making is anything but the invention of something that has never existed? Anyone who makes fictions, creates what are logical arguments — namely causes, effects, subjects, adjuncts, contraries, comparisons, or the rest of those things which originate from these. In this way Ovid, feigning the realm of the sun, feigned an efficient cause by which it was constructed, matter out of which it was put together, and adjuncts by which it was decorated. But feigning causes, effects, subjects, adjuncts and all the other arguments, is nothing other than inventing causes, effects, subjects, adjuncts. Therefore, fiction-making will be the same as the invention of something that does not yet exist. But if this is so, then the art of fiction-making will pertain not to poetry, but to dialectical invention, through which are conceived not only true things, but fictions as well. I grant that those things that are feigned belong to another discipline, to ethics, for the most part, or natural philosophy, no less than those arguments that are evident in the natural realm and which thrive there. But this very fiction-making, just like the thinking through of these arguments, is the action of either inborn or artificial thought in inventing. When Aristotle, therefore, defines poetry as a "fiction-making,"

Aristoteles poesin fictione definit, collocat poesin velut in domicilia
logicae inventionis violata lege καθάυτό. Ac proinde quoties fingunt
poetae, non id faciunt aliquo proprio munere poeseos sed dialec-
ticae artis facultate. |f. 12ᵛ|
Nam quod *Docere* & *Delectare* fines poeseos Ar[is]toteles esse vult, vult
hercle id quod in altero non est κ[α]θάυτό, in altero non est καθόλου
πρῶτον. facultas docendi, cum argumentis enuntiato, syllogismo,
methodo disposit[is] contineatur non erit poeseos sed dialecticae:
ideoque in poeseos definitione neutiquam καθάυτό. *Delectatio* etsi
potest a poetica suavitate proficisci, tamen manat etiam aliunde:
nempe a tropis, a figuris in repetitione soni & illis sententiarum,
ab actionis dignitate, ab inventionis subtilitate & elegantia, a judicii
sapientia & gravitate. *Delectare* igitur in poesi definienda non est
καθόλου πρῶτον. Quocirca laus poeticae facultatis e definitione
Aristotelica nulla est.
Quid e Distributione? qualis est?

Distributio poeseos e subjectis est.

Poesis posita est in exprimendis summi Dei excellentiis vel in explicatione philosophiae vel in iis imitandis fingendisque quae nunquam
extiterunt.
Non est distributio ista καθόλου πρῶτον. Nam & logicae disciplinae
facultas non minus quam poesis in hiis omnibus exercetur. Deinde
si poesis sit ars fictionis, non persequetur Summi Dei excellentias:
non in tractatione philosophiae versabitur. Etenim & illae excellentiae & res philosophicae vere existunt: non sunt commentitiae nec
igitur καθάυτό distributio est.

Prior distributionis pars duobus adjunctis exornatur: altero quod pro-
betur ab omnibus: altero quod adhiberi possit in laetitia & dolore.

De secunda ambigere videris sitne pars poeseos: quia materia huic
parti proposita non est quiddam cogitatione fictum. Ejusdem
argumenti jure de priore membro licuit dubitare: cum Dei excellentia
non sit e rerum fictarum numero.

he puts poetry, as it were, in the house of logical invention, mixing these two disciplines.[26] And just as often as poets feign, they do so not by some gift peculiar to poetry, but by the faculty of the art of dialectic.

Now because Aristotle wants teaching and delighting to be the ends of poetry, he certainly wants that which, for the first of these, mixes different disciplines, and for the other, fails to deal with the most general aspects of delight.[27] The faculty of teaching, since it is made up of arguments disposed by axiom, syllogism, and method, will belong not to poetry, but to dialectic. In this respect, then, the definition fails to deal with the essence of poetry itself. Even if delight can proceed from the sweetness of poetry, nevertheless it also flows from other places, such as from tropes, from figures in the repetition of sound and from those of wise sayings, from stateliness of delivery, from subtlety and elegance of invention, from wisdom and gravity of judgment. To define poetry by "delight," then, fails to deal with delight in its most general aspect. Thus the praise of the faculty of poetry from Aristotle's definition is null.

What can be said of the distribution of poetry? Of what sort is it?

The distribution of poetry is from its subjects.

Poetry consists either in expressing the excellences of God the Highest, or in explaining philosophy, or in imitating and figuring forth those things that have never existed.

Your distribution fails to take the most general aspects of the subject first, for certainly the faculty of logic is no less engaged than is poetry in all these things.[28] Moreover, if poetry should be an art of fiction, then it will not be describing the excellences of God the Highest, nor will it be engaged with matters of philosophy. For surely both these excellences and these matters of philosophy truly exist; they are not lies, and therefore, this distribution is internally inconsistent.[29]

The first part of the distribution, of divine poetry, is embellished through two adjuncts: the first concerns what should be argued from all such poetry; the other concerns what could be of use either in joy or sorrow.

As for the second part of the distribution, philosophical poetry, you seem to ask whether it is a part of poetry at all, since the matter proposed in this part is not some imagined fiction. But from this same argument one could rightly have wondered about the first part of this distribution, since God's excellence is also not numbered among fictional subjects.

Tertia pars illustratur dissimilitudine: Magnum (inquis) discrimen est inter hanc tertiam & illam secundam. |f. 13|

Dissimilitudinem Similium comparatione exornas:

Quale discrimen est inter mediocrem & excellentem pictorem: Tale est inter illam secundam & hanc tertiam poeseos partem. Protasin dissimili utriusque pictoris actione seu actionis subjecto declaras.

Ad uberiorem redditionis explicationem subjicis descriptionem tertiae partis. Descriptio est

e finibus: quod doceat & delectet.

e diversis:[6] quod non exprimat rem existentem sed fictam.

ex adjuncto: quod digni hii sint nomine poetae. id quod Simili doces: ut enim illi primi sunt digni appellatione Vatis: sic hii Poetae nomine. apodosin notatione confirmas conclusa enthymemate:

ποιοῦσι. itaque merito appellantur ποιηταί.

Anteced. ib. for these in deed. habet exornationem e fine. sed hîc subjicis finium e finibus explicationem climace rhetorico comprehensam.

Tertiam poeseos partem persequeris adhuc exposita distributione ipsius.

poetae in rebus fingendis occupati alii sunt ⎧ Heroici. Lyrici.
⎨ tragici. Comici.
⎬ satyrici. iambici.
⎩ elegiaci. bucolici.

Unde distributio haec sumpta sit ostendis. Ais sumi partim e subjecta materia quam tractant, partim ex adjuncto apparatu quo vestiri poemata sua voluerunt. Non placet haec (clarissime Sidneie) poetae distributio. in legitima distributione affectio partium ad totum unica erit non duplex. at in proposita distributione poetae facis duplicem

The third part of poetry is explained through an unlikeness: there is a great difference (you say) between this third part and the second. You ornament the unlikeness through a comparison of likes:

> Whatever distinction exists between a mediocre and an excellent painter;
>
> It is the same as that which exists between that second and this third part of poetry.

You express the first term of this comparison through the unlikeness of the performance, or of the subject of the performance, of each of these painters.

To explain the second term of this comparison more fully, you add a description of the third part of poetry. The description is:

> from final causes: that it teaches and delights;
>
> from differences: that it does not express what exists, but rather what is fictional;
>
> from the adjunct: that these are worthy the name of "poet," which you teach from comparison: just as that first kind of poet is worthy of the name *vates*, so these, the name "poet." You confirm the second term of this comparison by etymology, argued by enthymeme:
>
>> They make; therefore they are rightly called "poets" [makers].
>>
>> Antecedent: "for these indeede doo meerely make to imitate, and imitate both to delight and teach, and delight to moue men to take that goodnes in hande, which without delight they would flye as from a stranger" (159). This is embellished from final cause, but in this antecedent you add an explanation of final causes from final causes, set out in a rhetorical climax.[30]

You now carry on with the third part of poetry from the distribution set up earlier:

Poets concerned with feigning things are either	heroic; lyric
	tragic; comic
	satyric; iambic
	elegaic; bucolic

You show from where this distribution has been taken: you say it is taken partly from the subjects these poets treat, and partly from the adjunct of the metrical apparatus in which they have wanted their poems to be "dressed." This distribution of the poet (most noble Sidney) is not good enough. In a proper distribution, the affect relation of the parts to the whole will be single, not double.[31] But in the distribution of poets you propose, you make the relation of the

relationem partium ad totum, alteram subjecti, adjuncti alteram. Deinde e subjecti varietate genera poetarum distinguere non magis licet quam e rei explicandae dissimilitudine differentes species dialecticorum efficere. Dialecticus praecepta artis suae exercet modo in rebus heroicis & excellentissimis personis, modo in levioribus & minutioribus: nonnunquam |f. 13ᵛ| in reprehensione virtutum & vitiorum: interdum in re rustica: aliquando in amatoriis. Ecquid si quis ita dialecticum distribuat ut dicat alium heroicum esse tragicumve tractantem scilicet res gravissimas & eventu admirabiles: alium Comicum, disserentem nempe de levioribus pe[r]sonis: alium Satyricum, invehentem nimirum in hominum vitia: alium Bucolicum, disputantem videlicet de agro & bove: alium elegiacum, texentem amatoria: ecquid (inquam) hujusmodi distributio probaretur? Quod si dialecticus possit hoc modo distribui, peccat in legem καθόλου πρῶτον poetae distributio: in qua non poetae propria & germana membra sed partes dialectico cum ipso communes explicantur. si dialectici ejusmodi distributio vitiosa sit, non erit poetae distributio satis accurata. Nam ut eadem dialectici facultate res illae tractantur, etiamsi aliae ab aliis dissideant: sic, utcunque magna rerum dissimilitudo sit, eadem tamen poetae facultate tractantur universae. Accuratior est illa poetae distributio e poetici numeri differentia.

Postquam poetam in species tribuisti, disseritur abs te utrum oratio numeris astricta sit adjunctum ornamentum poeseos an pars ⌜essentialis⌝.[7] Doces versum esse poeseos vestimentum duntaxat non partem essentialem. argumentum est ab adjuncto versuum. concluditur enthymemate. integer syllogismus talis est e primo Connexi modo.

Si multi poetae extiterunt qui nunquam versu utebantur, & multi versu usi sunt qui non erant poetae: versus erit vestimentum poeseos non essentialis pars.

At multi poetae fuerunt qui nunquam versu utebantur, & multi versu usi sunt qui non erant poetae.

Itaque versus est vestimentum duntaxat poeseos non essentialis pars. |f. 14|

Propos. omit.

Assump. ib. Since there have been.

parts to the whole double, one relation concerning the subject, the other the adjunct. Furthermore, to distinguish kinds of poets through differences in their subjects is no more to be allowed than to create different species of logicians through differences in what they are to explain. A logician sometimes uses the principles of his art for heroic matters and most excellent personages; sometimes in lighter and smaller things; sometimes in correcting virtues and vices; occasionally in rustic things; at other times in amorous ones. And if anyone were to distribute the logician in this way, he would say that one kind is heroic or tragic, treating matters which are weighty and worthy in their outcome; another is comic, dealing, that is, with lighter personages; another is satiric, inveighing, obviously, against men's vices; another bucolic, holding forth about fields and cattle; another elegaic, weaving amorous things. But (I ask) however could such a distribution be accepted? Because if the logician could be distributed in this way, then your distribution of the poet would fail, since you can only use one such distribution.[32] What would be explained in such a distribution would not be the proper and common kinds of poet, but rather those kinds that are common to this same logician. But if on the other hand such a distribution of the logician is wrong, your distribution of the poet will still not be good enough. For just as those matters above are all dealt with through the same single faculty of the logician, even if some should be unlike others, similarly, however great the differences between poetry's subjects should be, they are all treated together through the same faculty of the poet. The distribution of the poet based on differences in poetic meter is more exact.[33]

After you have distributed the poet in species, you then ask whether metered verse is an ornamental adjunct to poetry or an essential part. You maintain that verse is only the vestment of poetry and not an essential part. The argument is from the adjunct of verse. It is concluded in an enthymeme. The whole syllogism is as follows, from the first mode of the connexive syllogism:

If many poets have existed who never used verse, and if many men have used verse who were not poets, then verse will be the vestment of poetry, and not an essential part.

But there have been many poets who never used verse, and many have used verse who were not poets.

Therefore verse is only the vestment of poetry, and not an essential part.

Proposition: omitted.

Assumption: "sith there haue beene many most excellent Poets that

Conclus. ib. Verse being but an ornament.

Assumptionis prior pars e specialibus exemplis probationem habet
dispositis syllogismo contracto.
   Xenophon & Heliodorus nunquam versu utebantur.
   Xenophon & Heliodorus sunt poetae.
   Quidam igitur poetae nunquam versu utebantur.
Propos. ib. yet both these wrote in prose.
Assump. & ib. for Xenophon. & ib. So did Heliodorus.
Conclus. ib. Since there have been many.

Erit dignitatis tuae de Assumptionis falsitate confiteri, si modo verum
fuerit fictionem esse propriam Dialectici non poetae.

Probatum est ab adjuncto versum esse duntaxat vestem poeseos: Idem
conaris e Similium collatione.
   Ut toga talaris causidicum non constituit:
   Sic nec versus poetam.
Agnosco ut in caeteris omnibus sic in hac quaestione magnum acumen
& subtilitatem. attamen quod nobilissimis & sapientissimis aliquando
contigit, interdum aberrat a Veritate oratio tua. Affers simili-
tudinem: sed reipsa dissimilitudo est, si dimensione soni comprehenditur natura poeseos. id quod necesse est esse, si fictione non
includitur.

Protasis e Diversis distinctionem habet. Etsi causam dicit armatus,
erit tamen causidicus.
Apodosis idem e Diversis distinguitur. Non versus sed illa imaginum
fictio naturam poetae notat. ubi finem attexis, ad docendum scilicet
cum delectatione. |f. 14ᵛ|
Disputata jam quaestione de versu sitne duntaxat vestis poeseos, objectioni respondes. Cur igitur (dixerit al[i]quis) poetae utuntur versu? Vis huic quaestioni satis fieri e contracta comparatione
Minorum: quae si explicetur suis partibus, erit hujusmodi:

neuer versified, and now swarme many versifiers that neede neuer aunswere to the name of Poets" (160).

Conclusion: "verse being but an ornament and no cause to Poetry" (159–60).

The first part of the Assumption is demonstrated from special examples, set out in a contracted syllogism:

Xenophon and Heliodorus never used verse.

Xenophon and Heliodorus are poets.

Certain poets, therefore, never used verse.

Proposition: "yet both these writ in Prose" (160).

Assumption: both "For *Xenophon*, who did imitate so excellently as to giue vs *effigiem iusti imperii*," and "so did *Heliodorus* in his sugred inuention of that picture of loue in *Theagines* and *Cariclea*" (160).

Conclusion: "sith there haue beene many most excellent Poets that neuer versified, and now swarme many versifiers that neede neuer aunswere to the name of Poets" (160).

Should it be true that fiction belongs to the logician, and not to the poet, it will be characteristic of your nobleness to admit that this Assumption is false.

It has been demonstrated from the adjunct that verse is only the cloak of poetry. You now try to do the same from a comparison of likes:

As a judicial robe does not make a lawyer;

So verse does not make a poet.

As in everything else, so in this question I recognize great skill and subtlety. Nevertheless, even if your discourse[34] sometimes deals with the most noble and most wise, it sometimes strays from the truth. You suggest a likeness, but if the essential nature of poetry is comprised by meter — which would necessarily follow if poetry is not defined as a fiction — then there is in fact an unlikeness.[35]

The first term of the comparison is made clear from differences. Even if he pleads his case in armor, he will still be a lawyer.

The second term of the comparison is similarly made clear from differences: not verse, but the feigning of images characterizes the nature of the poet. To this argument you add the final cause, that it is, of course, for teaching with delight.

Having already argued the question of whether verse is only the cloak of poetry, you respond to an objection. Why then (someone might ask) do poets use verse? You want to take care of this question with a contracted comparison from the lesser, which, if it is laid out in its parts, will be like this:

> Oratio numeris soluta est vestis perapta.
>
> At oratio numeris astricta est vestis aptissima.
>
> respondes etiam objectioni e fine adhibitae vestis: ut nempe caeteris omnibus vestimenti genere poetae antecellant. finis iste habet amplificationem e Simili:
>
> Ut poetae vincunt caeteros dignitate materiae:
>
> Sic etiam eisdem praestare volunt genere vestimenti.

Finis porro e Diversis ostenditur. ib. Not speaking table. Propositio similitudinis minus vera erit si materia vere existens sit fictae par dignitate aut superior.

Postquam tertiam poeseos partem & descripseris & distribueris ais non alienum esse si ipsam ex effectis, deinde e partibus explices, eum ad finem ut illi laudem concilies. Ornas igitur poetam ab effectis conclusis secunda specie syllogismi explicati.

Quod nos ad faelicitatem optime ducit, id princeps est caeterarum artium. ib. those skills that.

Poesis nos optime ad faelicitatem ducit. ib. Wherein yf we can.

Poesis igitur est princeps caeterarum artium. ib. Even the man that.

Assumptionem illustras collatione Minorum:

> Reliquae artes conantur nos ad faelicitatem ducere: ib. This puri.
>
> At poeta id optime facilimeque praestat. ib. wherein yf we.

Protasin inductione confirmas judicata enthymemate.

> Prose is excellent clothing.
> But verse is more excellent.

You also reply to this objection from the final cause of the cloak that is used, namely, that poets should excel all others in the ways they dress their matter. This final cause is amplified from likeness:

> Just as poets excel others in the dignity of their matter;
> So they also want to excel others in the kind of cloak they use.

Then this final cause is shown from an argument of differences: "not speaking (table talke fashion or like men in a dreame) words as they chanceably fall from the mouth, but peyzing each sillable of each worde by iust proportion according to the dignitie of the subject" (160). The Proposition of this simile will be less true if a truly existing subject should either equal or surpass a feigned subject in dignity.[36]

After describing and distributing this third part of poetry, you say that it will not be amiss if you were to explain this same sort of poetry from effects and then from parts in order to win praise for it. Thus you embellish the poet from effects, argued through a full syllogism of the second figure:

Whatever leads us best to felicity, that is the prince of all the other arts: "those skilles that most serue to bring forth that haue a most iust title to bee Princes ouer all the rest" (161).

Poetry leads us best to felicity: "Wherein if wee can shewe the Poets noblenes, by setting him before his other Competitors" (161).

Poetry therefore is the prince of all the other arts: "euen the man that ought to carry the title from them both, and much more from all other seruing Sciences" (163).

You illustrate the Assumption of this syllogism by a comparison from the lesser:

> The other arts try to lead us to felicity: "This purifing of wit, this enritching of memory, enabling of iudgment, and enlarging of conceyt, which commonly we call learning, vnder what name soeuer it com forth, or to what immediat end soeuer it be directed, the final end is to lead and draw vs to as high a perfection as our degenerate soules . . . can be capable of" (160).

> But the poet excels in this best and most readily: "Wherein if wee can shewe the Poets noblenes, by setting him before his other Competitors" (161).

You confirm the first term of this comparison by an induction disposed in an enthymeme:

Astronomia, physica, Musica, mathematica conantur nos ad
faelicitatem perducere. ib. This according.
itaque reliquae artes ib. This purifying of Wit. |f. 15|
Antecedentem enthymematis exornas e Diversis:
Etiamsi Astronomia caeteraeque artes id conantur: Sunt tamen
administrae facultates. ib. Then loe did.
Illas artes esse administras facultates probatur ex adjuncto errore. ib.
But when by the. Deinde est amplificatio e Simili:
Ut illae artes habent suum & proprium finem.
Sic referuntur ad summum finem.

Redditionis exornatio est e definitione Architectonices. finem in definitione comprehensum demonstras e Simili.

Assumptionem principis syllogismi vidimus illustratam collatione
Minorum & exornatam prosyllogismis suis. Assumptionis secundum
argumentum est e Disparatis primo modo syllogismi disjuncti
conclusis.

Aut ethicus aut historicus aut jureconsultus aut poeta nos ad
faelicitatem ducit facilime.
At non ethicus nec historicus nec jureconsultus nos ad faelicitatem ducit
facilime.
Itaque poeta id praestat.
Propos. ib. And those fower ar all.[8]
Assump. ib. But both not having. & ib. And for the lawier.
Conclus. ib. Wherin yf We can.
Assumptio constat e tribus partibus. priusquam earum ulla tractatur,
proponis nobis descriptionem & ethici & historici: alterumque cum
altero velut disputantem inducis de via ad virtutem.

Astronomy, physics, music, mathematics, try to lead us to felicity: "This, according to the inclination of the man, bred many formed impressions" (160).
Therefore the other arts do too: "This purifing of wit . . ." (160).
You embellish the enthymeme's first term from differences:
Even if astronomy and the other arts try to lead us to felicity, nevertheless they are serving sciences: "then loe, did proofe, the ouer ruler of opinions, make manifest that all these are but seruing Sciences" (161).

That those arts are serving sciences is shown from the adjunct of error: "But when by the ballance of experience it was found that the Astronomer looking to the starres might fall into a ditch" (161). Next is an amplification from simile:
As these arts have a private end in themselves;
Similarly, those ends are all directed to the highest end.

The second term of this comparison is embellished from the definition of "Architechtonic."[37] From simile you show the final cause of all arts [i.e., "well dooing and not . . . well knowing onely" (161)] to be implicit within this definition.

We have seen the Assumption of the main syllogism above [i.e., "Poetry leads us best to felicity"] illustrated by a comparison from the lesser, and embellished through its prosyllogisms. A second argument dealing with this Assumption is from disparates, argued in a disjunctive syllogism of the first mode:

Either the moral philosopher, the historian, the lawyer, or the poet leads us to felicity most readily.
But neither the philosopher, nor the historian, nor the lawyer leads us to felicity most readily.
Therefore the poet does it.
Proposition: "And these foure are all that any way deale in that consideration of mens manners" (164).
Assumption: "But both not hauing both, doe both halte" (164); and: "And for the Lawyer . . . because hee seeketh to make man good rather *Formidine poenae* then *virtutis amore*" (163).
Conclusion: "Wherein if wee can shewe the Poets noblenes, by setting him before his other Competitors" (161).
The Assumption has three parts. Before you deal with any of them, you propose for us a description of the philosopher and the historian; you introduce one as if he were arguing with the other about the path to virtue.[38]

Ethici descriptio est primum ex adjunctis, scilicet:
    gravitate quadam morosa: quae arguitur e fine, nempe ad
    testandum odium vitii.
    agresti apparatu: qui declaratur etiam e fine, ad significan-
    dum contemptum rerum externarum. |f. 15^v|
    libellorum gestatione in manibus: quae exponitur & e sub-
    jecto libellis explicato, nimirum disputatione contra gloriam:
    & adjuncta inscriptione nominis.
Deinde[9] ex effectis:
    Sophistice contra subtilitatem loquitur.
    Irascitur iis, in quibus iracundiam animadvertit.
    Definit, dividit, distinguit.
Ethicus sic descriptus disputat de expeditissima ad virtutem via: quam
    probat ethica disciplina contineri. argumentum affert e subjecto.
    Quae ars virtutem tractat, ea expeditissimam viam continet ad
    virtutem. ib. Whether it be possibl[.]
    Ethica virtutem tractat. omittitur velut notissima.
    Ethica igitur continet Viam expeditissimam ad virtutem. ib.
    Among Whom as princi.
Atque haec est ethici descriptio & disputatio.

Historicus describitur
    e subjectis, in quibus legendis se exercet. ib. but y^t he load[.]
    ex adjuncta difficultate tollendae inter historias dissension[is.]
    e duplici comparatione. ib. Better acquaynted.
    ex adjunctis. ib. Curious for antiquities.
    ex effectis. ib. A Wonder to young. Nam efficere admirationem
    & in consuetudine communis sermonis velut regnum quaerere
    sunt effecta.
    denique ex adjuncta ira & ostentatione. ib. Denieth in a great
    chafe.

The description of the moral philosopher is first from adjuncts, namely:

> from a certain sullen gravity, argued from final cause, i.e., to reprove the evil of vice;
>
> from his rude clothing, which is also explained from final cause, i.e., to show contempt for outward things;
>
> from his carrying little books in his hands, which is explained both from the subject dealt with in these books, i.e., from their making arguments against glory; and from the adjunct of his setting his own name to these works.

Then he is described from effects:

> He speaks sophistically against subtlety.
>
> He is angry with those in whom he sees anger.
>
> He defines, divides, distinguishes.

The moral philosopher so described holds forth about the most ready path to virtue, which he argues is contained in the discipline of ethics. He makes his argument from the place of subject:

> Whatever art treats virtue, that art holds the most ready path to virtue: "whether it bee possible to finde any path so ready to leade a man to vertue as that which teacheth what vertue is" (162).
>
> Ethics treats virtue. (This is omitted as well-known.)
>
> Ethics therefore holds the most ready path to virtue: "among whom as principall challengers step forth the morrall Philosophers" (161).

And that is the description and the argument of the moral philosopher.

The Historian is described:

> from the subjects of those things he spends his time reading: "but that he, loden with old Mouse-eaten records" (162);
>
> from the adjunct of the difficulty of clearing up disagreement between histories ["hauing much a-doe to accord differing Writers" (162)];
>
> from a double comparison: "better acquainted with a thousande yeeres a goe then with the present age, and yet better knowing how this world goeth then how his owne wit runneth" (162);
>
> from adjuncts: "curious for antiquities and inquisitiue of nouelties" (162);
>
> from effects: "a wonder to young folkes and a tyrant in table talke" (162), since its effects are to create wonder and to seek, as it were, for a kingdom in the habits of common conversation;
>
> finally, from the adjunct of anger and ostentation: "[he] denieth,

Historici disputatio de expeditissima ad virtutem via nititur argumento
subjecti enthymemate dispositi.
  Historia suppeditat exempla quibus docetur virtus.
  Historia igitur commonstrat expeditissimam viam ad virtutem.
|f. 16|
Antecedentem enthymematis in specie explicat varia comparatione
  Dissimilium. ubi concludit historicus se praestare omnibus
  philosophis. argumentum est e subjecto disciplinae historicae.
  Multorum annorum usus superat omnes philosophorum libellos.
    ib. Old aged experience.
  Ego (inquit histor) multorum annorum usum suppedito. ib. But
    J give.
  Ego igitur sum omnibus philosophis praeferendus.
porro antecedentem enthymematis probat ab effecto:
  Historia senatores & principes erudivit ad virtutem. ib. Then
    would he alleag.
  Historia itaque exemplis virtutem docet.

Ad confirmationem antecedentis subjiciuntur exempla Bruti & Alphon-
si, id est, argumenta speciei.

Habemus jam ethici & historici disputationem de via ad virtutem expeditissima. Nunquid & hic & ille quod voluit assecutus est? certe
in demonstratione expeditissimae ad virtutem viae uterque claudicat.
Quem igitur in isto negotio principem dicemus? Poeta (inquis) utrique palmam praeripit.
  Hîc e Comparatione Majorum doces a poesi omnes alias administras scientias in hoc negotio superari.
    Poeta superat ethicum & historicum.
    Multo igitur magis alios administros artifices.
  Antevertis objectionem de theologia. fateris excipiendam esse.
    argumentum est e majoribus: quorum notae sunt, non solum
    sed etiam.

in a great chafe, that any man for teaching of vertue, and vertuous actions, is comparable to him" (162).

The historian's case for the most ready path to virtue depends on an argument from subject, set out in an enthymeme:

History supplies examples through which virtue is taught.
History thus shows the most ready path to virtue.

The historian sets out the first term of this enthymeme in species through a multiple comparison of unlikes, where he concludes that he excels all philosophers. The argument is from the subject of history:

The experience of many ages is more important than all the books of the philosophers: "Olde-aged experience goeth beyond the fine-witted Phylosopher" (163).
I (the historian says) make the experience of many ages available: "but I giue the experience of many ages" (163).
I am thus to be preferred to all the philosophers.

Then he argues the enthymeme's first term from effect:

History has led senators and princes to virtue: "Then would hee alledge you innumerable examples, conferring storie by storie, how much the wisest Senatours and Princes haue beene directed by the credite of history" (163).
History therefore teaches virtue by examples.

The examples of Brutus and Alphonse are added to confirm this first term. It is, that is, an argument of species.

We now have the case of the philosopher and historian for the most ready path to virtue. Has either one attained what he wanted? Surely each of them limps in showing the most ready path to virtue, so which shall we say is the prince in this? The poet (you say) takes the prize from both of them.

Here you explain by a comparison from the greater that in this matter poetry also surpasses all the other serving sciences:

The poet surpasses the moral philosopher and the historian;
Much more, then, the other serving sciences.

You anticipate an objection from theology: you admit that theology is to be excluded. The argument is from a comparison from the greater and its terms are set out in a "not only . . . but even" construction ["as for the Diuine, with all reuerence it is euer to be excepted, not only for hauing his scope as far beyond any of these as eternitie exceedeth a moment, but euen for passing each of these in themselues" (163)].

Verumenimvero Poetae principatum in hoc negotio urges vehementius & concludis. Redis igitur ad disjuncti syllogismi assumptionem ⟨convellendam⟩ demonstrandam. |f. 16ᵛ|

Disjuncti syllogismi assumptio ait nec ethicum nec historic[um] nec jureconsultum facilime nos ad faelicitatem ducere.

Primo jureconsultum aggrederis & refellis e fine juris civilis.

> Jureconsultus solummodo cavet ne homo homini noceat.

> Non est igitur iis artificibus conferendus qui extirpata nequitia serunt in hominum mentibus virtutem.

Anteced. ib. And for the lawier.

Conclus. ib. Therfore as our Wickedness. illustratur e Diversis & collatione Similium.

De enthymematis antecedente vix assentietur jureconsultus. Dicet enim se non modo de prohibenda injuria sed etiam de virtute colenda praecipere.

A jureconsulto discedis ad ethicum: quem e Materia ethicae disciplinae refutas:

> Ethicus solummodo praeceptum tradit de faelicitate.

> Ac proinde non aeque facile nos ad faelicitatem ducit ac ille qui & praecepto & exemplo ad faelicitatem erudit.

Anteced. ib. The one by praecept. deductam ex antecedente consequentiam ab adjuncta obscuritate traditae disciplinae demonstras.

Obscuritas traditae disciplinae declaratur efficiente:

> Ethica praecepta sunt generalibus & abstractis notionibus comprehensa. ib. for his knowledg.

> Sunt igitur obscura. ib. for the philosopher.

Quod ethicus solummodo praeceptum tradat de faelicitate, in eo hominis peccatum est non artis. Nam ethica recte descripta & omnibus instructa membris cum praecepta tum exempla continet quibus ad faelicitatem erudiamur. si quis vulgarem ethicen intueatur, illa

Then surely you plead with great force and argue for the poet's dominion in this business. Thus you turn again to demonstrating the Assumption of the earlier disjunctive syllogism.

The Assumption of the disjunctive syllogism says that neither the moral philosopher nor the historian nor the lawyer leads us most readily to felicity.

First you deal with the lawyer and you make your refutation from the final cause of civil law.

> The lawyer only takes care that one man should not harm another.
> He is therefore not to be placed among those makers, who, with wickedness rooted out, plant virtue in men's minds.

Antecedent: "And for the Lawyer. . .[he] dooth not indeuour to make men good, but that their euill hurt not others" (163).

Conclusion: "Therefore, as our wickednesse maketh him necessarie, and necessitie maketh him honorable, so is hee not in the deepest trueth to stande in rancke with these who all indeuour to take naughtines away, and plant goodnesse" (163–64). This is illustrated both from differences and from a comparison of likes.

With respect to the Antecedent of this enthymeme, the lawyer will hardly agree. He will surely say that he teaches not just about preventing injury, but also about cultivating virtue.

From the lawyer you move on to the moral philosopher, whom you refute from the subject of ethics:

> The moral philosopher teaches only the precept of felicity.
> Therefore he does not lead us to felicity as readily as one who teaches the path to felicity by both precept and example.

Antecedent: "the one by precept" (164). You demonstrate the consequence deduced from this first term through the adjunct of the obscurity with which this discipline is delivered. The obscurity of the discipline's delivery is set forth from the efficient cause:

> Ethical precepts are bound up in general and abstract notions: "for his knowledge standeth so vpon the abstract and generall" (164).
> They are, therefore, obscure: "For the Philosopher, setting downe with thorny argument the bare rule, is so hard of vtterance" (164).

When a moral philosopher treats only the precept of happiness, this is a failure of the man, not the art. For rightly described and set out in all its parts, ethics contains not only precepts but examples as well through which we should be instructed how to achieve felicity. If someone should look to an ordinary treatment of ethics, then perhaps it does not teach about felicity through the illuminations

fortasse non adhibitis exemplorum luminibus de faelicitate praecipit: perinde ut jurisprudentia tantummodo de prohibenda injuria praeceptum dat. Verum ut in arte jurisprudentiae sic in ethica doctrina non quid jam praestetur attendimus |f. 17| sed quid praestari debeat quidque in rei natura positum sit spectamus.

obscuritatis, quae inest in ethica disciplina, demonstratio a generalibus ducta theorematis non magis valet contra ethicen quam contra poeticam caeterasque artes quarum praecepta generale aliquid complectuntur.

Ethico refutato disseris adversus historicum: idque a subjecto historiae concluso enthymemate.

Historicus nos exempli alicujus & rerum particulari veritate erudit. ib. On the other side the historian.

Itaque minus utilem disciplinam continet. ib. And therfore a less.

Enthymematis consecutionem illustras ab exempli adjuncta inconsequentia.

Hactenus syllogismi disjuncti assumptio tractata est. Quid ergo? Sane vero si e tribus illis nemo est, qui nos ad faelicitatem ducit facilime, sequitur poetam eum esse, a quo id praestatur. Huc tu contendis nervos ingenii tui, ut illam de poetae tam excellenti actione conclusionem demonstres. Primum argumentum fuit a Disparatis: secundum sequitur ab effecto poetae.

Qui & praecepto & exemplo virtutem docet, is nos ad faelicitatem ducit facilime.

At poeta & praecepto & exemplo virtutem docet.

Poeta igitur nos ad faelicitatem ducit facilime.

Propos.[10] deest.

Assump. ib. Now doth the peerles. declaratur effecto.

Poeta exhibet perfectam imaginem ejus rei, de qua facienda philosophus praecipit. ib. for whatsoever.

Itaque praeceptum cum exemplo conjungit. ib. So as he coupleth.

Ruere & assumptionem & assumptionis illustrationem necesse est, si of examples, just as law only gives a precept forbidding wrong-doing. But just as in the art of law, so in the teachings of ethics, we consider not what is now being offered, but we look to what ought to be offered, and at whatever makes up the nature of something.[39]

Your demonstration of the obscurity which exists in ethics, inferred from the universals of its theory, is no more fittingly argued against ethics than against poetry and other arts whose precepts deal with any general thing.[40]

With the moral philosopher refuted, you turn to the historian. What you say is from history's subject, shown in an enthymeme:

> The historian teaches us through the particular truth of some example or set of circumstances: "On the other side, the Historian, wanting the precept, is so tyed, not to what shoulde bee but to what is, to the particuler truth of things and not to the general reason of things" (164).

> Therefore he has a less useful discipline: "and therefore a lesse fruitfull doctrine" (164).

> You illustrate the way this enthymeme follows logically by observing from the place of adjunct that a single example has no necessary consequence.[41]

So far you have been treating the Assumption of the earlier disjunctive syllogism, and why? Surely because if none of these three professions leads us most readily to felicity, it follows that the poet is the one by whom this task is performed. Here you exert your powers of wit to demonstrate your conclusion concerning the poet's so very excellent performance. The first argument was from disparates; the second follows from the poet's effect:

> Whoever teaches virtue through both precept and example, he leads us most readily to felicity.

> But the poet teaches virtue both through precept and example.

> The poet therefore leads us most readily to felicity.

Proposition: omitted.

Assumption: "Nowe dooth the peerelesse Poet performe both" (164).

It is set out from effect:

> The poet shows the perfect image of that thing which the philosopher teaches should be done: "for whatsoeuer the Philosopher sayth should be doone, hee giueth a perfect picture of it in some one, by whom he presupposeth it was doone" (164).

> Therefore he joins precept with example: "So as hee coupleth the generall notion with the particuler example" (164).

If my case against your definition of poetry and about the perfection

& contra poeseos definitionem & de ethicae disciplinae perfectione
vere disputatum est.
                                                                    |f. 17ᵛ|
Atque hîc occurritur prolepsi. Objici enim potest, etiamsi poeta perfectam imaginem rei jam factae exhibet, plus tamen ad docendu[m]
valere praeceptionem philosophiae. Doces ergo ad docendum plus
valere perfectam imaginem poetae quam praeceptum philosophi.
argumentum est ab effecto poeticae imaginis dispositum
enthymemate.
            Quod hominis mentem vehementius afficit, id ad docendum
            valet plurimum.
            Imago depicta a poetis hominis mentem vehementius afficit
            quam praeceptum philosophi.
            Ac proinde imago depicta a poetis valet plurimum ad
            docendum.
        Prop.[11] omit.
        Ass. ib. for he yeldeth.
        Con. ib. for the quaestion.
Assumptio habet exornationem e similibus.
        Protas. ib. for as in outward.
        Apod. ib. so no doubt.   \

Est etiam alia assumptionis amplificatio e duplici inductione
    specialium. prior est e prophanis. ib. Let us but hear old Anchises.
    in disputatione hujus inductionis duplex prolepsis refellitur, altera
    de Mori Eutopia, altera de poeta a philosophis victo. refutationis
    argumentum utrobique, est e Diversis. Est (inquis) vitium hominis
    non poetae.
        Posterior inductio est e theologia. ib. Certaynly even our saviour
        Christ. ubi exponitur efficiens causa proponendarum imaginum,
        nempe vis expressae imaginis ad movendum nota Christo &
        explorata.

of ethics has been rightly argued, then it is necessary to do away both with this Assumption, and with its illustration.[42]

At this point you deal with a possible objection to your Assumption. For someone can object that even if the poet shows the perfect image of an action already done, the precept of philosophy still has more force for teaching. In response, you explain that the perfect image of the poet has more force for teaching than the philosopher's precept. The argument, from the effect of the poetic image, is set out in an enthymeme:

> Whatever affects a man's mind most strongly has the most force for teaching.
>
> The image painted by poets affects a man's mind more strongly than does the precept of the philosopher.
>
> Therefore the image painted by poets has the most force for teaching.

Proposition: omitted.

Assumption: "for hee yeeldeth to the powers of the minde an image of that whereof the Philosopher bestoweth but a woordish description" (164).

Conclusion: "for the question is, whether the fayned image of Poesie or the regular instruction of Philosophy hath the more force in teaching" (166).

The Assumption is embellished from a comparison of likes:

Protasis: "For as in outward things, to a man that had neuer seene an Elephant or a Rinoceros" (164–65).

Apodosis: "so no doubt the Philosopher with his learned definition" (165).

There is a further amplification of the Assumption from a two-fold induction of specials. The first is taken from the profane poets: "Let vs but heare old *Anchises* speaking in the middest of Troyes flames" (165). In arguing this induction you answer two possible objections, one concerning More's *Utopia*, the other concerning the poet's being bettered by the philosopher. The argument of the refutation to both objections is from differences. It is, you say, a vice of the man, not of the poet.

The second induction is from theology: "Certainly, euen our Sauiour Christ could as well haue giuen the morrall common places of vncharitablenes and humblenes as the diuine narration of *Diues* and *Lazarus*" (166). Here the efficient cause of the images to be set forth is made clear, namely, the power of an expressed image to move, a power that Christ understood and put to proof.

Tandem quaestionem istam dissimilitudine philosophi & poetae in docendo concludis.
    Propos. ib. for conclusion.
    Reddit. ib. But the poet. |f. 18|
    Redditionem arguis e specie. ib. Wherof Aesops fables.
Ab ista quaestione ad objectionem refutandam digrederis. objectio concluditur tali syllogismo.
    Imago rei verae plus ad docendum valet quam fictae.
    Historicus proponit imaginem rei verae, Poeta imaginem rei fictae.
    Historicus igitur plus ad docendum valet quam Poeta.
Propositionem hujus syllogismi refellis exposito subjecto utriusque imaginis. syllog. explicat. secund. spe.
    Praeceptum de formanda ad excellentissimam ideam actione plus valet ad docendum quam narratio rei hoc illove modo factae.
    ib. But yf the quaestion.
    At poetarum imago continet praeceptum formandae actionis ad excellentissimam ideam: historicorum imago narrat quid actum fuerit. ib. W^{ch} the poesy considereth.
    Ergo poetica imago plus ad docendum valet quam vera.
Conclusionis prosyllogismus est ab efficiente facilitatis in docendo, conclusa enthymemate.
    Poeta rem καθόλου considerat, historicus καθέκαστον.
    Poeta igitur est historico aptior ad docendum.
Anteced. ib. His reason is because.
Con. ib. Poetrye is φιλοσοφώτερον.

Finally you conclude this question with an unlikeness between the philosopher and the poet in teaching.

> Proposition: "For conclusion, I say the Philosopher teacheth, but he teacheth obscurely" (167).
>
> Reddition: "but the Poet is the foode for the tenderest stomacks, the Poet is indeed the right Popular Philosopher" (167).

You argue this second term from species: "whereof *Esops* tales giue good proofe" (167).

From this question you pause to answer an objection. That objection is set out in the following syllogism:

> The image of something true has more force for teaching than the image of something feigned.
>
> The historian sets forth an image of something true; the poet an image of something feigned.
>
> The historian thus has more force for teaching than the poet.

You answer the first term of this syllogism by having set out the subject of each image. The argument is disposed in a full syllogism of the second figure:

> Teaching that concerns shaping action to a most outstanding idea has more force for teaching than the recounting of something that has actually been done one way or another: "But if the question be for your owne vse and learning, whether it be better to haue it set downe as it should be, or as it was, then certainely is more doctrinable the fained *Cirus* in *Xenophon* then the true *Cyrus* in *Iustine*" (168).
>
> But the poets' image contains precepts concerning the shaping of action to a most outstanding idea, while the historians' image recounts what was done: "which the Poesie considereth in his imposed names" (167).
>
> The poetic image therefore has more force for teaching than the true image.

One prosyllogism of this conclusion is from the efficient cause of facility in teaching, concluded in an enthymeme:

> The poet considers a thing universally, the historian particularly.
>
> The poet therefore is more suited for teaching than the historian.

Antecedent: "His reason is, because Poesie dealeth with *Katholou*, that is to say, with the vniuersall consideration; and the history with *Kathekaston*, the perticuler" (167).

Consequent: "Poetry is *Philosophoteron* and *Spoudaioteron*, that is to say, it is more Philosophicall and more studiously serious then history" (167).

Ethicae praeceptionis cujusdam obscuritatis supra coarguebantur
quia generalibus erant comprehensae notionibus. At hoc loco
poeta, quia rem in genere non singillatim in specie considerat,
ideo aptior esse dicitur ad docendum quam poeta. Si rerum
generalis consideratio probatur in poeta, non debet in ethicae
disciplinae magistro improbari.

Conclusionis prosyllogismus alter est e similibus.
> Protas. ib. As to a Ladie.
> Apodo. ib. But yf the quaestion. |f. 18ᵛ|

propositio objectionis refutata hactenus est e subjecto ut[ri]usque imaginis. refutatur jam ab effecto poetae.
> Poeta quid in exemplis sequendum fugiendumque sit exponens
> judicium nostrum in actionibus conformat. ib. yf yᵉ poet.
> Itaque ficta poetarum imago plus ad docendum valet quam
> historicorum vera.

Porro ad laudem historiae etiam alia quaedam adversus poesin objiciuntur. Primum ejusmodi est.
> In historica rei gestae narratione major authoritas est ad consimilis
> facti imitationem quam in poetica fictione.
> Historiae igitur imago est praeferenda poeticae.

Enthymematis antecedentem negas. negationis argumentum est ab adjuncto: quia in historico exemplo est probabilis duntaxat ratio ad
persuadendum hominibus de consimilis facti imitatione. Ad hujus
probationem affertur fortunae effectum conclusum enthymemate:
> Fortuna nonnunquam hominum consilia & prudentiam antever-
> tit. ib. Where the historian.
> itaque facti imitatio probabili duntaxat ration[e] nititur. ib. But
> yf he know.

Earlier, ethics was accused of a certain obscurity in its teaching because it was made up of universal notions.[43] But here, the poet, because he considers things universally, and not singularly in species, is said for that reason to be more suited for teaching than the historian. But if considering things through universals is to be approved of in the poet, it ought not to be condemned in a teacher of ethics.

The conclusion's other prosyllogism is from a comparison of likes:

> Protasis: "As to a Lady that desired to fashion her countenance to the best grace, a Painter should more benefite her to portraite a most sweet face" (168).

> Apodosis: "But if the question be for your owne vse and learning. . .certainely is more doctrinable the fained *Cirus* in *Xenophon* then the true *Cyrus* in *Iustine*" (168).

So far the first term of the earlier objection has been refuted from the subject of each kind of image. Now it is refuted from the poet's effect:

> The poet, showing in examples what is to be followed or shunned, shapes our judgment in what we do: "If the Poet doe his part a-right, he will shew you in *Tantalus, Atreus,* and such like, nothing that is not to be shunned; in *Cyrus, Aeneas, Vlisses,* each thing to be followed" (168).

Thus the feigned image of the poets has more force for teaching than the the true one of the historians.

Next, in praise of history certain other things are objected against poetry. The first is of this kind:

> There is in the historical narration of an event more authority for the imitation of a similar action than there is in a poetic fiction ["the historie, in his saying such a thing was doone, doth warrant a man more in that he shall follow" (168)].[44]

Therefore the historical image is to be preferred to the poetic image.

You deny the first term of this enthymeme. The negation is from the adjunct, since in a historical example there are only probable grounds to persuade men to the imitation of a similar action. To show this, you use the effect of fortune, argued by enthymeme:

> Fortune sometimes overrules men's counsels and wisdom: "where the Historian in his bare *Was* hath many times that which wee call fortune to ouer-rule the best wisedome" (168).

> Therefore the imitation of an action depends solely on probable grounds: "but if he know an example onlie informes a coniectured likelihood, and so goe by reason, the Poet dooth so farre

Deinde non modo fortunae effecto sed etiam adjuncto historicarum
actionum res proposita explicatur: quod scilicet multarum actionum
nullae causae, nisi fictitiae[,] reddi possunt.
Ad tuendam fictae causae explicationem disputas ficta exempla ad
docendum aeque valere ac vera. argumentum est a specie.
Xenophontis fictus Abradates aeque nos in honestae dissimilationis
genere erudit ac Justini Zopyr[us.]
Ficta igitur exempla aeque ad docendum valent ac vera.|f. 19|
E Xenophontis fictione concludis historicum esse subjectum Poetae.
Quaecunque consilia & stratagemata ab historico narrantur, ea
possunt a poeta tractari ornarique. ib. for whatsoever.
itaque subjicitur poetae historicus. ib. so then.

Antecedentis posterior pars de poeta declaratur e tractationis & fine
& subjecto. finis ib. beautifying it both. subjectum ib. having all
from Dante. Quo loco prolepsin e Diversorum distinctione diluis.
Nullus poeta (dixerit aliquis) hoc praestitit.
Non loquor (inquis) de homine sed de arte.

Secundum ex aliis illis, quae ad laudem historiae ad versus poesin
objiciuntur, est praeclara quaedam cognitio nata ex eventorum
observatione una cum incitatione mentis ad summum bonum.
Quomodo istud refellitur? Ad prioris refutationem vera causa tam
praeclarae cognitionis exponitur judicata enthymemate:
Poeta est author hujus tam praeclarae cognitationis. ib. Truly that
com.
Non igitur historicus. ib. And far from history.[12]

Utcunque aliquid ab historico aut in tradenda nobis excellenti cogni-

exceede him, as hee is to frame his example to that which is most reasonable" (168).

Moreover, this matter is explained not only by the effect of fortune, but also by the adjunct of the actions that the historians describe, since unless they are fictional, no causes for many actions can be given.

To defend this explanation about such a fictional cause, you argue that fictional examples have as much force for teaching as true ones.[45] The argument is from species:

Xenophon's feigned Abradates teaches us as much about honest dissimulation as the Zophyrus of Justine.

Fictional examples thus have as much force for teaching as true ones.

From this argument based on Xenophon's fiction you conclude that the historian is subject to the poet.

Whatever counsels and strategies are narrated by the historian, they can be treated and beautified by the poet: "for whatsoeuer action, or faction, whatsoeuer counsell, pollicy, or warre stratagem the Historian is bound to recite, that may the Poet (if he list) with his imitation make his own" (169).

Thus the historian is subject to the poet: "So then the best of the Historian is subiect to the Poet" (169).

The second part of this enthymeme's first term, concerning the poet, is set out both from the final cause and from the subject of the work. From the final cause: "beautifying it both for further teaching, and more delighting" (169); from the subject: "hauing all, from *Dante* his heauen to hys hell, vnder the authoritie of his penne" (169). At this point you weaken a possible objection by an argument from differences:

No poet (someone might say) has actually excelled in this.

I do not speak (you say) of the man, but of the art.

The second of these other arguments brought against poetry and in praise of history has to do with a kind of notable learning that comes from an observation of events together with a moving of the mind towards the highest good. How is that argument answered? To refute the first clause of this attack, the true cause of so notable a learning is set out, disposed in an enthymeme:

The poet is the author of so notable a learning: "Truely that commendation is peculiar to Poetrie" (170).

Not, therefore, the historian: "and farre of from History" (170).

Although something may be achieved by the historian either in fur-

tione aut incitanda mente ad summum bonum praestetur. Vincitur
tamen in utroque a poeta: ut constat ex effectis poetae ⌈& historici⌉
conclusis enthymemate.

Poeta accendit in hominum animis amorem Virtutis odiumque
vitii, historicus vero a virtute saepissime deterret hortaturque
ad vitium.

Praestat itaque historico poeta utraque re.
Prop. deest.
Assump. ib. for in deed poetry. & ib. But the history.
Conclus. ib. J conclude therfor.　　　　　　　　　　　　　　|f. 19ᵛ|

Contra assumptionem illud afferi potest nimirum hortationem ad
vitium non esse historiae, sed hominis de quo historia loquitur.
Deinde quae ad defensionem Comediae abs te deinceps afferuntur
(nam quod adversus comaediam idem adversus historiam objicitur)
ea possunt ad tuendam historiam commodissime transferri: adeo
ut alio loco historiae infligas plagam, alio inflictae plagae medearis.
⌈Porro poetam esse solum authorem tam praeclarae cognitionis
historicus pernegabit.¹¹³

Assumptionis prima pars de poeta probatur adjuncto virtutis & vitii.
　　　Virtus & vitium a poeta eleganter ad oculum depinguntur. ib. for
　　　　in deed. & ib. And of the.
　　　Poeta igitur accendit in hominum animis amorem virtutis odium-
　　　　que vitii.
Virtutem vitiumque sic depingi disseritur argumento speciei.
　　　Patientia & animi magnitudo sic a poetis depinguntur.
　　　Patientia & animi magnitudo sunt virtutes.
　　　Quaedam igitur virtutes sic depinguntur.
Prop. ib. Wel may we se Ulisses.¹⁴
Assump. deest.
Conclus. ib. for in deed.
Virtutis vitiique effigiem eminentem fateor a poetis proponi nobis ob
　　　oculos. sed effigiei istius prima lineamenta omnesque colores, quibus

nishing us with excellent learning, or in moving the mind towards the highest good, nevertheless, in each of these he is surpassed by the poet. This is clear from the effects of the poet and the historian, concluded by enthymeme:

The poet stirs in men's minds the love of virtue and the hatred of vice; the historian, however, very often discourages virtue and encourages vice.

The poet thus surpasses the historian in each of these.

Proposition: omitted.

Assumption: "For indeede Poetrie euer setteth vertue so out in her best cullours" and "But the Historian, beeing captiued to the trueth of a foolish world, is many times a terror from well dooing, and an incouragement to vnbrideled wickednes" (170).

Conclusion: "I conclude, therefore, that hee excelleth Historie" (171).

One can certainly argue against your Assumption by saying that it is not history that encourages vice; rather it is the man about whom the history speaks. Moreover, the same things you use to defend comedy (for the same thing is objected against comedy as against history) can in turn be very nicely transferred to the defense of history.[46] To the extent you wound history in one argument, you heal the wound in another. And the historian will deny absolutely that the poet is the only author of such notable learning.

The first part of the Assumption, dealing with the poet, is argued from the adjunct of virtue and vice.

Virtue and vice are very elegantly portrayed to the eye by the poet: "For indeede Poetrie euer setteth vertue so out" and "And of the contrarie part, if euill men come to the stage" (170).

The poet therefore stirs in men's souls a love of virtue and a hatred of vice.

That virtue and vice are portrayed like this is made clear by an argument of species:

Patience and magnanimity are portrayed this way by poets.

Patience and magnanimity are virtues.

Thus some virtues are portrayed this way.

Proposition: "Well may you see *Vlisses* in a storme, and in other hard plights; but they are but exercises of patience and magnanimitie" (170).

Assumption: omitted.

Conclusion: "For indeede Poetrie euer setteth vertue so out" (170).

I grant you that poets set before our eyes a noble image of virtue and vice. But the essential features of this image, and all the colors by which it is varied and differentiated, are the arguments of logical

variatur & distinguitur, sunt logicae inventionis argumenta vestita rhetoricis ornamentis.

Assumptionis secunda pars de historico disputatur & e causa efficiente & tractationis subjecto.

Efficientem historicae cohortationis ad vitium facis explicandae veritatis necessitatem.

Tractationis subjectum concluditur enthymemate: |f. 20|
  Historia proponit nobis viros praestantes calamitate oppressos, improbos vero rebus secundis utentes.
  Historia igitur deterret a virtute & hortatur ad vitium.
Propos. omit.
Assump. ib. for see we not. ubi inductio specialium loco assumptionis adhibetur.
Conclu. ib. But the history.

Potes eodem argumento (ornatissime Sidneie) Comaediam & tragaediam criminari: immo & Odisseam Homeri, in qua Ulisses vir excellenti virtute afficitur vario genere calamitatum.

Adhuc tractata est assumptio sillogismi illius, qui e poetae & historici effectis concluditur.

Conclusio duas habet partes: alteram de tradenda nobis cognitione: alteram de incitanda mente ad summum bonum.

Conclusionis posterior pars habet exornationem e Majoribus. ib. W^ch setting forward. deinde e Diversis. ib. for suppose it be. Diversorum posterior pars de principatu poetae in facultate movendi tractatur uberius.

Quaeritur ergo an poeta vincat philosophum movendi facultate. ab effecto poetae concluditur vinci philosophum a poeta. Syllog. expli. secund. sp.
  Qui maxime movet ad cognoscendum & ad praxin rei cognitae, is philosophum caeterosque vincit facultate movendi. ib. But to be moved.
  At poeta maxime movet ad cognoscendum & ad praxin rei cognitae. ib. Now therin of all sciences.

invention, dressed in rhetorical ornaments.[47]

The second part of the Assumption dealing with the historian is argued both from the efficient cause and from the subject of the work.

The efficient cause of the history's encouragement of vice you take to be the need to tell the truth.

The work's subject is argued in an enthymeme:

History sets before us excellent men oppressed by calamity, and wicked men actually enjoying good fortune.

History therefore discourages virtue and encourages vice.

Proposition: omitted.

Assumption: "For see wee not valiant *Milciades* rot in his fetters?" (170), where an induction of specials is used in place of the Assumption.

Conclusion: "But the Historian, beeing captiued to the trueth of a foolish world, is many times a terror from well dooing, and an incouragement to vnbrideled wickednes" (170).

Through this same argument (most noble Sidney) you can criticize comedy and tragedy, and even Homer's *Odyssey*, where Ulysses, a man of excellent virtue, is afflicted with several sorts of calamities.

So far the Assumption of the earlier syllogism has been dealt with; the syllogism argues its conclusion from the effects of the poet and the historian.

The Conclusion has two parts: the first deals with furnishing us with knowledge; the second with moving the mind to the highest good.

The second part of the Conclusion is embellished through a comparison from the greater: "which setting forward, and moouing to well dooing, indeed setteth the Lawrell crowne vpon the Poet" (171). Then from an argument of differences: "For suppose it be granted (that which I suppose with great reason may be denied) that the Philosopher, in respect of his methodical proceeding, doth teach more perfectly then the Poet" (171). The last part of this argument of differences, concerning the poet's mastery in moving, is treated more fully.

Thus you ask whether the poet surpasses the philosopher in the capacity to move. From the poet's effect you conclude that the poet does indeed surpass the philosopher. The argument is in a full syllogism of the second figure:

He who moves most both to knowing and to doing what is known, surpasses the philosopher and all the rest in the capacity to move: "but to be moued to doe that which we know, or to be mooued with desire to knowe, *Hoc opus, hic labor est*" (172).

But the poet moves most to knowing and to doing what is known: "Nowe therein of all Sciences (I speak still of humane, and according to the humaine conceits) is our Poet the Monarch" (172).

Poeta igitur philosophum vincit facultate movendi. ib. yet do J
   think that. |f. 20ᵛ|
Propositionem arguis e Minoribus contracta comparatione inclusis.
Movere est quiddam excellentius quam docere. Co[m]paratio plena
sic erit. Docere est excellens quiddam: at Movere longe excellen-
tius. Comparatio ista confirmat[ur] adjuncto concluso
enthymematicōs. integer syllogismus addita propositione ejusmodi
est. secund. spe. expl.
   Causa & effectum docendi superat dignitate ipsum Docere.
   Movere est causa & effectum Docendi.
   Movere igitur superat dignitate ipsum Docere.
Prop. deest.
Assump. ib. it may appear.
Concl. ib. And yᵗ moving.

Utcunque de causa docendi concedatur vincere eam dignitate ipsum
   Docere: certe idem de effecto docendi non concesserim. Nam si effectum consideremus habita duntaxat relatione ad causam, erit
quidem in eo ipso, quatenus a causa procreetur, vel eâdem inferius
dignitate vel ad summum par. peccat itaque propositio. Quod si
motus non sit causa Docendi, erit etiam minus legitima assumptio.
Sevoca argumenta enuntiato, syllogismo, methodo disposita a motu:
nunquam hercle a motu docebere. quod tamen eveniret, si motus
esset docendi causa. Eo solum docemur, quod menti cognitionem
aliquam tradit. at hoc non ullo motu sed vi & lumine argumenti
ad judicii regulas dispositi tantum efficitur. Ecce porro, si vere a
te isto syllogismo disseritur, non tam motus actioni docendi
praeferetur quam motui actio docendi. Causa superat dignitate ipsum effectum: id quod e syllogismi tui propositione colligitur. At
Docere est causa, movere effectum Docendi, ut est in Assumptione.
sequetur ergo ut docendi actio superet motum dignitate. |f. 21|

Assumptio declaratur e Relatis parium collatione tractatis: nempe
   assumptionis prima pars de causa Docendi.

The poet therefore surpasses the philosopher in the capacity to move: "yet do I thinke that no man is so much *Philophilosophos* as to compare the Philosopher, in moouing, with the Poet" (171). You argue the Proposition from a contracted comparison from the lesser: Moving is a thing more excellent than teaching. The full comparison will be as follows: Teaching is an excellent thing, but moving is far more excellent. This comparison is confirmed by the adjunct, concluded in an enthymeme. The whole syllogism, with the Proposition added, would be as follows, in a full syllogism of the second figure:

> The cause and the effect of teaching are of a higher degree than teaching itself.
> Moving is the cause and the effect of teaching.
> Moving, therefore, is of a higher degree than teaching itself.

Proposition: omitted.
Assumption: "it may by this appeare, that it is wel nigh the cause and the effect of teaching" (171).
Conclusion: "And that moouing is of a higher degree then teaching" (171).

While it may be conceded that the cause of teaching is to be valued more highly than teaching itself, certainly I would not concede the same for the effect of teaching.[48] For if we should consider effect only in terms of the relation it holds to cause, then since an effect is itself produced by a cause, it will in fact be either inferior to its cause, or equal at best. Thus your Proposition is wrong. But if moving should not even be the cause of teaching, then your Assumption will be even less legitimate than your Proposition. Keep the issue of "moving" distinct from that of arguments disposed by axiom, syllogism, and method. Certainly you will never be taught just by moving; yet that would be the case if moving were the cause of teaching. We are only taught by that which brings about some sort of knowledge in the mind; yet this does not happen by any "moving," but only by the force and illumination of an argument, ordered through the rules of judgment. Observe, then, that if you set this syllogism of yours out properly, moving is not so much to be valued above the act of teaching, as the act of teaching is to be valued above moving. A cause has more value than its effect — as the Proposition of your syllogism makes clear. But teaching is a cause, and (as you state in your Assumption) moving is its effect. Thus it will follow that teaching is of a higher degree than moving.

The Assumption is set out from relatives, treated through a comparison of equals. Surely its first part concerns the cause of teaching:

Movere est causa discendi. ib. for who wilbe taught.
Movere igitur est causa docendi. ib. it may appeare.
si causam, qua impellimur allicimurve ad discendum, intelligis, assentior de antecedente enthymematis. sed quaeritur (credo) non de causa, qua invitamur ad docendum & discendum, sed de causa, qua velut gignitur & formatur in hominis mente cognitio. illam in motu, hanc in argumentis colloco: non tamen sic, tanquam illa causa, qua allicimur ad discendum, sola esset author discendi. Nam & argumentorum condere atque elegantia adducimur ad discendum.

[A]ssumptionis secunda pars de effecto Docendi explicatur ⟨effecto⟩ conjugati argumento.
  Docendo movemur ad id agendum quod docetur.
  itaque motus est effectum docendi.
Anteced. ib. And what so much.
Concl. ib. it may appear.[15]
Antecedente comprehensum effectum illud docendi exornatur comparatione Minorum: quod nempe ex omnibus docendi effectis, illud Movere ad agendum sit praestantissimum. plena comparatio erit hoc modo:
  Multa sunt praeclara docendi effecta.
  At Movere ad agendum est longe optimum.
Comparatio Minorum ib. And what so much good. demonstrationem ab effecto habet.
  Non pervenimus ad praxin absque motu ad praxin.
  Jtaque motus ad praxin erit effectum docendi praestantissimum.
Anteced. ib. And how praxis.
Conseq. ib. And what so much. |f. 21ᵛ|
Ad ⟨Assumptionem⟩ ⌜Antecedentem⌝ firmandam adhibetur adjunctum judicatum enthymemate.
  Ad fructum vitae non pervenitur absque motu.

Moving is the cause of learning: "For who will be taught, if hee bee not mooued with desire to be taught?" (171).

Moving, therefore, is the cause of teaching: "it may by this appeare, that it is wel nigh the cause and the effect of teaching" (171).

If you understand a cause here to be what urges or attracts us to learning, I agree to the first term of the enthymeme. But the question, I think, is not of the cause by which we are invited to teaching and learning, but of the cause by which knowledge is begotten and formed, as it were, in someone's mind. The first I put in moving, the second in arguments; still, I do not make this allocation of causes as if that cause by which we are attracted to learning should be the only source of learning. For we are also attracted to learning through the making of arguments and through eloquence.

The second part of the Assumption, dealing with the effect of teaching, is explicated through an argument from the conjugate:

By teaching we are moved to doing what is taught.

Therefore, moving is the effect of teaching.

Antecedent: "and what so much good doth that teaching bring forth (I speak still of morrall doctrine) as that it mooueth one to doe that which it dooth teach?" (171).

Conclusion: "it may be this appeare, that it is wel nigh the cause and the effect of teaching" (171).

The effect of teaching described in the Antecedent is embellished further by a comparison from the lesser: surely of all the effects of teaching, the most outstanding is its moving to action. The full comparison will look like this:

There are many outstanding effects of teaching.

But moving to action is by far the best.

The comparison from the lesser: "and what so much good doth that teaching bring forth . . . as that it mooueth one to doe that which it dooth teach?" (171). This is shown from effect:

We do not come to action without being moved to action.

Moving to action will thus be the most outstanding effect of teaching.

Antecedent: "And howe *Praxis* cannot be, without being mooued to practise, it is no hard matter to consider" (171).

Consequent: "and what so much good doth that teaching bring forth . . . as that it mooueth one to doe that which it dooth teach?" (171).

To support the Antecedent you use an adjunct, disposed in an enthymeme:

The fruit of life is not achieved without being moved.

Praxis est fructus vitae.
Ad praxin igitur non venitur absque motu.
Propos. deest.
Ass. ib. for as Aristotle.
Con. ib. And how praxis.[16]
Assumptio e Diversis distinguitur, not γνῶσις but πρᾶξ[ις,] ubi est
    testimonium Aristotelis.

Accedit etiam antecedenti firmitas ex alio adjuncto.
    Cognitio viae ad faelicitatem ducentis absque ardenti studio non
        prodest ad praxin.
    Ad praxin igitur absque motu ad praxin non pervenitur.
Prop. omitt.
Assump. ib. But this to noe man.
Concl. ib. And how praxis.
    Assumptio est duarum partium: altera de cognitione viae ad
        faelicitatem: altera de ardenti studio.
    Cognitio viae ad faelicitatem arguitur ab efficiente duplici,
        philosopho nempe & natura. Nam & ille & haec tradit cogni-
        tionem viae. ib. The philosopher. & ib. Since in nature wee.
    Ardens studium commendatur e pari: quod hominem in via illa
        conficienda tantum adjuvet, quantum e philosophorum libellis
        cognitio.

Hactenus syllogismi principis propositio, qua dicitur ab eo, qui max-
    ime movet ad cognoscendum & ad praxin rei cognitae, vinci
    philosophum facultate movendi, est prosyllogismis disputata suis.
|f. 22|Restat Assumptionis prosyllogismus. Assumptio ait poetam max-
    ime movere ad cognoscendum & ad praxin rei cognitae. hujus
    demonstratio est ex effectis comparatis.
    Poeta non modo viam ostendit ad faelicitatem sed etiam inserit
        in hominum animis mirificam cupiditatem progrediendi ad eam.

Action is the fruit of life.

Action, therefore, is not achieved without being moved.

Proposition: omitted.

Assumption: "for, as *Aristotle* sayth, it is not *Gnosis* but *Praxis* must be the fruit" (171).

Conclusion: "And howe *Praxis* cannot be, without being mooued to practise, it is no hard matter to consider" (171).

The Assumption is divided by differences: "not *Gnosis* but *Praxis*," where the division is from the testimony of Aristotle.

The force of the Antecedent is made even stronger through another adjunct:

Knowledge of the way that leads to felicity does not bring about action except by ardent study.

Thus, without being moved to action, one does not act.

Proposition: omitted.

Assumption: "But this to no man but to him that will read him, and read him with attentiue studious painfulnes" (171).

Conclusion: "And howe *Praxis* cannot be, without being mooued to practise, it is no hard matter to consider" (171).

The Assumption has two parts. One deals with knowing the way to felicity, the other deals with ardent study.

Knowing the way to felicity is argued from two efficient causes, namely, from the philosopher and from nature, since both these deal with knowing the way: "The Philosopher sheweth you the way" (171), and "seeing in nature we know it is wel to doe well, and what is well and what is euill" (172).

You give ardent study a place of importance through a comparison of equals, since it helps a man make his way just as much as the knowledge that comes from the books of the philosophers ["Which constant desire, whosoeuer hath in him, hath already past halfe the hardnes of the way" (171)].

So far, the Proposition of the principal syllogism, where it is said that whoever moves most to both knowing and to doing what is known surpasses the philosopher in the ability to move, has been argued through its prosyllogisms.

What remains to be discussed is the prosyllogism of the Assumption. The Assumption says that the poet moves most to knowing, and to doing what is known. The demonstration of this is from a comparison of effects:

The poet not only shows the way to felicity, he also plants in men's souls a wonderful desire to follow that way.

Poeta igitur in movendo est facile princeps.

Anteced. ib. for he doth not only.

Conse. ib. Now therin of all. repetitur ib. By these therfor.

Ad antecedentis probationem afferuntur efficientes tam praeclarae
cupiditatis: nempe in ipso aditu, verborum concinna & elegans com-
positio, harmonica incantatio, fabula tantarum virium ut & pueros
a lusu & senes a somno detineat.

Axioma istud causas complexum tam excellentis cupiditatis
amplificatur

    E similibus. ib. Nay he doth as yf.

    E Diversis. ib. he beginneth not wth.

    E fine. ib. And p'tending noe more.

Finis iste comparatione Similium exornatur:

    Protas. ib. Even as the child.

    Apod. ib. So is it in men.

Apodosin efficiente doces, nempe poetica imitatione quae est naturae
nostrae familiaris.

Poeticam imitationem, cui cum natura nostra cognatio quaedam in-
tercedit esse tantae delectationis efficientem constat

    Primum e testimonio Aristotelis. ib. Jn so much that.

    deinde specialibus exemplis. ib. Truly J have knowen.

    tum effecto philosophorum. [ib.] wch Plato and Boetius.|f. 22^v|

The poet is thus easily the Monarch in moving.

Antecedent: "For he dooth not only show the way, but giueth so sweete a prospect into the way, as will intice any man to enter into it" (172).

Consequent: "Nowe therein of all Sciences (I speak still of humane, and according to the humaine conceits) is our Poet the Monarch" (172). This is repeated: "By these, therefore, examples and reasons, I think it may be manifest that the Poet, with that same hand of delight, doth draw the mind more effectually then any other Arte dooth" (174–75).

To prove the Antecedent you give the efficient causes of so noble a desire, namely, a polished and elegant setting out of words, even as the work begins; a harmonious enchanting music; a tale of such strength that it keeps children from play and old men from sleep. This axiom dealing with the causes of so excellent a desire is amplified:

from similes: "Nay, he dooth, as if your iourney should lye through a fayre Vineyard, at the first giue you a cluster of Grapes" (172);

from differences: "He beginneth not with obscure definitions" (172);

from the final cause: "And, pretending no more, doth intende the winning of the mind from wickednesse to vertue" (172).

This final cause is embellished from a comparison of likes:

Protasis: "euen as the childe is often brought to take most wholsom things by hiding them in such other as haue a pleasant tast" (172).

Apodosis: "So is it in men" (172).

You explain the Apodosis of this comparison by its efficient cause, namely poetic imitation—which is natural to us.

That the efficient cause of such delight is poetic imitation, in which there occurs a certain affinity with our own nature, is made clear:

First from the testimony of Aristotle: "in somuch that, as *Aristotle* sayth, those things which in themselues are horrible, as cruell battailes, vnnaturall Monsters, are made in poeticall imitation delightfull" (173).

Then from special examples: "Truely, I haue knowen men, that euen with reading *Amadis de Gaule* (which God knoweth wanteth much of a perfect Poesie) haue found their harts mooued" (173).

Then from its effect on philosophers: "which *Plato* and *Boethius* well knew, and therefore made Mistres Philosophy very often borrow the masking rayment of Poesie" (173).

Effectum philosophorum illustratur efficiente, nempe imbecillitate
philosophiae ad delectandum & movendum, quae coegit ipsos
mutuari a poetis apparatum. finis mutuationis in delectando positus
declaratur e Diversis:
> Etsi refractarii & perditi homines monitis philosophorum non
> moventur:
> Tamen delectari se facile patiuntur.

Diversorum posterius membrum tractatur & effecto delectationis. ib.
And so ste[a]le to see. & Similium comparatione. ib. as yf they tooke.

Postremo ex aliis exemplis specialibus conclusis syllogismo contracto.
> Menenii Agrippae & Nathanis oratio perexcellentem delectationem
> habuit.
> Menenii Agrippae & Nathanis oratio erat imitatio poetica.
> itaque imitatio poetica vehementer hominum animos rapit
> afficitque.

Propos. ib. The one of Menenius. & ib. The other is of.
Ass. ib. But forsooth. & ib. But the Discourse it self.
Concl. ib. By these therfore examples.
Assumptio habet utroque loco distinctionem e Diversis.
Conclusio habet amplificationem e Minoribus. ib. More effectually
then any other art. ubi est conclusio argumenti ex effectis allati ad
poeseos ornandam laudem.

Laus poeseos ab effectis sic est. sequitur laus poeseos ab inductione
partium. Priusquam hoc argumentum persequeris, praefaris de in-

This effect on philosophers is illustrated by its efficient cause, namely, philosophy's weakness in delighting and moving, which forced
these same men to borrow devices from the poets. The purpose of
this borrowing, which is to delight, is stated in an argument from
differences:
> Even if stubborn and desperate men are not moved by the warn-
> ings of the philosophers;
> Nevertheless they readily allow themselves to be delighted.

The second member of this comparison of differences is dealt with both
from the effect of delighting ("and so steale to see the forme of
goodnes" [173]), and from a comparison of likes: "as if they tooke
a medicine of Cherries" (173).

Finally, you argue from other special examples set out in a contracted
syllogism:
> The speaking of Menenius Agrippa and of Nathan gave most ex-
> cellent delight.[49]
> The speaking of Menenius Agrippa and of Nathan was a poetic
> imitation.
> Poetic imitation thus strongly seizes and affects men's minds.

Proposition: "The one of *Menenius Agrippa*, who, when the whole people
of Rome had resolutely deuided themselues from the Senate, with
apparant shew of vtter ruine, though hee were (for that time) an
excellent Oratour, came not among them vpon trust of figuratiue
speeches or cunning insinuations" (174), and "The other is of *Nathan*
the Prophet, who when the holie *Dauid* had so far forsaken God as
to confirme adulterie with murther, when hee was to doe the
tenderest office of a friende . . . how doth he it but by telling of a
man whose beloued Lambe was vngratefullie taken from his bos-
ome?" (174).

Assumption: "but forsooth he behaues himselfe like a homely and
familiar Poet" (174), and "but the discourse it selfe fayned" (174).

Conclusion: "By these, therefore, examples and reasons, I think it may
be manifest that the Poet, with that same hand of delight, doth draw
the mind more effectually then any other Arte dooth" (174–75).

Both parts of the Assumption are set off through differences.

The Conclusion is amplified through a comparison from the lesser:
"more effectually then any other Arte dooth" (175), where the argument's conclusion is from effects, used to embellish the praise of
poetry.

That is how the praise of poetry from effects goes. Now follows praise
of poetry from an induction of parts, but before you go ahead with

stituenda |f. 23| singularum partium consideratione: eamque suades
e fine, ut nempe siquid naevi & labeculae sit in poesi, eo facilius
appareat. praefaris etiam de facta a nonnullis quarundam partium
conjunctione. ubi a pari disputas eam esse laudabilem.
  Si partes singulae separatim laudabiles sunt, aliae cum aliis
    conjunctae sunt laudabiles.
  At singulae partes separatim laudabiles sunt.
  Jtaque aliae cum aliis conjunctae sunt laudabiles.
Prop. ib. for yf severed.
Assumptio est singularum partium inductio conclusa sequenti
  syllogismo.
Concl. ib. But that cometh. & ib. Since all his knwdg.[17]
Sequitur ipsa partium inductio conclusa syllogismo connexo secundi
  modi.
Si poesis reprehendenda est, reprehendenda est aut Bucolica aut elegia
  aut iambica aut Satyra aut Comica aut tragica aut lyrica aut heroica.
At non Bucolica aut caeterarum partium ulla reprehendenda est.
Poesis igitur non est reprehendenda.

Assumptionis partes singulas separatim tractas: ac primo Bucolicam:
  cujus laudem e subjecto demonstras. Quinetiam caeteras poeseos
  partes vindicas e reprehensione notato subjecto tractationis. De Comoedia cum loqueris, defendis comicam imitationem e similibus:
    protas. ib. Now as in Geometry. apodos. so in the actions.
  deinde ab effectis. Nam docet comoediae & qui sint improbi &
    qualia sint facta improborum.
  Tum prolepsin de propositis in scena improbis refellis ab ⟨effecto⟩
    adjuncto odio visae nequitiae. Adjunctum istud arguitur effi-
    ciente, nempe |f. 23ᵛ| vi veritatis in natura: & Diversis: Quan-
    quam ipse se eisdem vitiis irretitum non intelligit: odit tamen
    vitia, quae in aliis videt.
Tragicae imitationis effectum in Alexandro Pheraeo notas.
Lyricas cantilenas non modo e subjecto sed etiam ab effecto commen-

this, you first discuss the setting up of such a consideration of single parts. You urge us to such a consideration from the final cause — in order, that is, that if any spot or blemish should exist in poetry, it should more easily be seen. Your introduction also comments on a conjoining made from some of these parts, where you argue from a comparison of equals that such a conjoining is laudable:

> If single parts are laudable separately, then they are laudable when some of them are joined together.
> But single parts are laudable separately.
> Thus they are laudable when some are joined together.

> Proposition: "for, if seuered they be good, the coniunction cannot be hurtfull" (175).
> Assumption: This is an induction made up of single parts, given in the syllogism below.
> Conclusion: "But that commeth all to one in this question" (175), and "Sith all his kindes are not onlie in their vnited formes but in their seuered dissections fully commendable" (181).

The induction of parts itself now follows, set out in a connexive syllogism of the second mode:

If poetry is to be censured, then either pastoral or elegy, iambic or satire, comedy or tragedy, lyric or heroic is to be censured.
But neither pastoral nor any other part is to be censured.
Poetry is therefore not to be censured.

You deal with each part of the Assumption separately, beginning with pastoral, whose value you show from its subject, but you also defend poetry's other parts against attack on any of their subjects. When you speak of comedy, you defend comic imitation through similes:

> Protasis: "Now, as in Geometry the oblique must bee knowne as wel as the right" (177). Apodosis: "so in the actions of our life who seeth not the filthines of euil wanteth a great foile to perceiue the beauty of vertue" (177).

> Then you defend comedy from effects, for it teaches both who the wicked men are, and what these men's deeds are like.

> Then you answer a possible objection about putting these wicked men on the stage, from the adjunct of hatred for the evil one sees there. This adjunct is argued from its efficient cause, namely from the force of truth in nature. You also argue from differences: although a man does not see that he is himself entangled in these same vices, he nevertheless hates the vices that he sees in others.

You note the effect of tragic imitation on Alexander Pheraeus.
You praise the old lyric songs not only from their subject, but also

das. ib. Certaynly J must confess. Tum ab efficientibus, Hungaris nimirum & Lacedaemoniis: quorum cantilenae e subjecto loco, e materia, e fine describuntur.

Prolepsin de Pindaro diluis e Diversis: Vitium erat hominis, temporis, graeculae consuetudinis non poeseos.

Graecula consuetudo in tanta aestimatione levissimarum rerum ostenditur e Philippi regis effecto.

Heroicam poesin non modo e subjecto sed e fine ornas. Nam ideo continet historiam clarissimarum virtutum, ut illarum amore accendamur.

deinde comparatione Minorum. quod scilicet sit praestantissimum genus poeseos. plena comparatio erit ejusmodi:

Aliae partes poeseos sunt praestantes.

At heroica poesis est praestantissima.

Apodosin effectis exaggeras: quod & mentem inflammet cupiditate excellentiae & eandem erudiat ad rationem consequendae excellentiae.

Heroicae poeseos effecta augentur e Simili: ib. for as the image. tum e speciali exemplo: ib. Only let AEneas. speciale exemplum ornas collatione Minorum: quod plus valeat quam praeceptum philosophi. ib. Melius Chrysippo.

Quod si igitur subjectum illud, quod a singulis poeseos partibus tractatur, in laude versetur: quis de laude singularum partium dubitaverit?

Poetae laudem concludis e similibus ad vituperatores poeseos, convincendos stultitiae.

Protas. ib. But truly J imagin.

Apod. ib. so the name of.

Est etiam totius laudationis, quam hactenus perpolivisti, |f. 24| ἀνακεφαλαιῶσις conclusa enthymemate.

from effect: "Certainly I must confesse my own barbarousnes: I neuer heard the olde song of *Percy* and *Duglas* that I found not my heart mooued" (178). Then you praise them from the efficient causes of poetry, in particular, among the Hungarians and the Lacedemonians, whose songs are described from where they were sung, from their matter, and from final cause.

You answer from differences a possible objection about Pindar, saying the fault was of the man, of the time, and of Greek custom, but not of poetry.

Greek custom in giving so much value to trivial things is illustrated from its effect on Philip of Macedon.

You embellish heroic poetry not only from subject but also from final cause, for it tells the history of most noble virtues in order that we should be inflamed with a love of them.

    Then you argue through a comparison from the lesser that heroic poetry is, of course, the most outstanding kind of poetry. The full comparison will be like this:

        Other parts of poetry are outstanding.
        But heroic poetry is most outstanding.

You magnify the comparison's second term through its effects, since heroic poetry both inflames the mind with a desire for excellence, and teaches the mind how to become excellent.

    The effects of heroic poetry are developed further from a comparison of likes: "For as the image of each action styrreth and instructeth the mind, so the loftie image of such Worthies most inflameth the mind with the desire to be worthy, and informes with counsel how to be worthy" (179). Heroic poetry's effects are then amplified with a special example: "Only let *Aeneas* be worne in the tablet of your memory" (179). You embellish this special example through a comparison from the lesser: Such an example has more force than the philosopher's precept: *"Melius Chrisippo et Crantore"* (180).

But if then that subject which is treated by each of poetry's parts is to be praised, who would doubt the value of each part?

You finish your praise of the poet by proving from arguments of likeness the dullness of poetry's critics:

    Protasis: "But truely I imagine it falleth out with these Poet-whyppers, as with some good women, who often are sicke, but in fayth they cannot tel where" (180).

    Apodosis: "So the name of Poetrie is odious to them" (180).

And now there is a recapitulation of all the praise you have thus far beautifully written, included in an enthymeme:

Anteced. ib. Since then poetry is of all.

Conseq. ib. J think (& J think.[18]

Hactenus (praestantissime Sidneie) veritatis confirmatio ad laudem poeseos tractata est: sequitur jam refutatio calumniae.

Antequam refutationem aggrederis, praefaris de audiendis & disceptandis iis, quae adversus poesin objici possunt: deinde de Scommatum levitate.

Auditio argumento instrumenti, disceptatio argumento adjuncti concluditur enthymemate:

Aures habemus aeque ac linguas: audire igitur oportet objecta.

Leuissima argumenta magni ponderis videbuntur esse, si nihil contra afferatur. oportet itaque quid contra dicatur expendere.

Antecedens utriusque enthy. ib. But because we have.

Conseq. ib. Let us hear & as well.

Scommatum indig.itas arguitur ex adjunctis: quod multis & inanibus verbis comprehendantur: & quod indigna sint quibus respondeatur. tum e subjectis: quod ad ludendas res singulas adhibeantur. deinde ab efficiente, quod nascantur e stultitia. Origo ista explicatur ex adjuncto nomine, quod Majores nostri ludibundis sycophantis imposuerunt.

A praefatione ad ipsam calumniam accedis. Quae ergo est prima calumnia? certe ejusmodi.

Rithmus & metrum sunt res stultae & leves.

itaque & poesis.

Huic enthymemati respondes negata consequentia: negatae consequentiae ratio est ab adjuncto: |f. 24ᵛ|

Poesis esse potest etiamsi removeantur rithmus & metrum.

Non sequetur ergo ex illorum labe labes poeseos.

Antecedent: "Sith then Poetrie is of all humane learning the most auncient and of most fatherly antiquitie, as from whence other learnings haue taken theyr beginnings" (180).

Consequent: "I think (and think I thinke rightly) the Lawrell crowne appointed for tryumphing Captaines doth worthilie (of al other learnings) honor the Poets tryumph" (181).

So far, most noble Sidney, you have been engaged in a confirmation of truth in praise of poetry. Now follows a refutation of calumny.

Before you begin your refutation, you introduce your discussion with a remark about hearing and pondering those things that can be objected against poetry, and then you remark on the lightness of jests made against poetry.

Listening is dealt with by an argument of instrument; pondering, by an argument of adjunct. Both are argued by enthymeme:

We have ears as well as tongues; we should therefore listen to objections.

The lightest arguments will seem of great weight, if nothing is brought against them. We should thus ponder what is said against poetry.

Antecedent for both enthymemes: "But because wee haue eares aswell as tongues, and that the lightest reasons that may be will seeme to weigh greatly, if nothing be put in the counter-ballance" (181).

Consequent: "let vs heare, and aswell as wee can ponder, what obiections may bee made against this Arte" (181).

The baseness of jests against poetry is argued from adjuncts: they are comprised of words that are both inane and too many, and they are unworthy of anything one might respond to them. Then from subjects: they are concerned to mock every single thing. Then from the efficient cause: they originate in foolishness. This origin is explained by the adjunct of the name our forefathers gave to such jesting sycophants [i.e., "great fooles" (182)].

After this preface you go on to the calumnies themselves. And what is the first of these?[50] Surely it goes like this:

Rhythm and meter are dull and laughable things;
Therefore, so is poetry.

You answer this enthymeme by denying the consequent. The basis for this denial is taken from the adjunct:

Poetry can exist even if rhythm and meter should be removed. Thus it will not follow from a blemish in rhythm and meter that poetry has blemishes.

Sed ecce quod ad poeseos reprehensionem affertur a sycophantis, in eo poeseos magnam laudem contineri doces. argument. est ab effect. conclus. syll. expli. secund.

Quod orationem ornat vocesque singulas numero & proportione expendit, laundandum est.
Poetica dimensio orationem ornat vocesque singulas numero & proportione expendit.
Laudanda igitur.
Prop. ib. That cannot be prayseles.
Ass. ib. But lay aside.
Con. ib. Truly it were.
Propositioni subjicis probationem ex adjuncto: quod videlicet oratio sit munus excellens.
Conclusionis prosyllogismus est ex effecto:
Quod magnopere juvat memoriam, laudandum est.
Poetica dimensio magnopere prodest memoriae.
ideoque laudanda.
Prop. omit.
Ass. ib. Now that verse far.
Con. ib. So that verse being.
Omissae propositionis loco confirmationem e subjecto posuisti:
Memoria[19] in rebus cognitis conservandis versatur.
Quod igitur juvat memoriam laudandum est.
Assumptio tractatur primum e Minoribus. ib. Now that verse far: ubi comparatur cum oratione soluta. tum e definitione poeticae dimensionis conclus. syll. expl. secund. |f. 25|

Verborum structura, qua verbum ex verbo velut gignitur & cujus levissima perturbatione memoria revocatur, memoriae vehementer conducit.
Poetica dimensio est hujusmodi verborum structura.
Poetica igitur dimensio conducit memoriae vehementer.

Propos. ib. The wordes (besides.

But then you show that even in this attack by its slanderers there is
great praise for poetry. The argument is from effect, organized in
a full syllogism of the second figure:

> Whatever polishes speech and considers each word by number
> and proportion is to be praised.
> Verse polishes speech and considers each word by number and
> proportion.
> Thus it is to be praised.

Proposition: "that can not be praiselesse which dooth most pollish that
blessing of speech, which considers each word, not only (as a man
may say) by his forcible qualitie but by his best measured quan-
titie" (182).

Assumption: "But lay a side the iust prayse it hath, by beeing the onely fit speech for Musick" (182).

Conclusion: "truelie it were an inseparable commendation" (182).

To the Proposition you add a proof from the adjunct: that "oratio"
is surely an excellent gift.

The prosyllogism of the Conclusion is from effect:

> Whatever greatly aids memory is to be praised.
> Verse greatly enhances memory.
> Thus verse is to be praised.

Proposition: omitted.

Assumption: "Now, that Verse farre exceedeth Prose in the knitting
vp of the memory" (182–83).

Conclusion: "So that, verse being in it selfe sweete and orderly, and
beeing best for memory, the onely handle of knowledge, it must be
in iest that any man can speake against it" (183).

In place of the omitted Proposition you have put a confirmation from
subject:

> Memory deals with retaining knowledge of things.
> Whatever aids memory is thus to be praised.

The Assumption is treated first through a comparison from the lesser:
"Now, that Verse farre exceedeth Prose" (182). There verse is compared with prose. Then the Assumption is dealt with from the definition of verse, given in a full syllogism of the second figure:

A structure of words by which one word grows, as it were, out of
another, and is recalled to memory by the slightest disorder, greatly aids memory.
Verse is this kind of verbal structure.
Therefore, verse greatly aids memory.

Proposition: "the words (besides theyr delight, which hath a great af-

Ass. ib. Be it in rime or measured.
Con. ib. Now that verse.

Deinde haec ipsa assumptio, quae illustratur e Minoribus & Definitione, aliam explicationem habet e causis adjuvantibus conclus. syll. expl. se.

Sedium & locorum distinctio valde confert memoriae.
Jn poetica dimensione est sedium & locorum distinctio.
Poetica itaque dimensio valde confert memoriae.

Prop. ib. Lastly even they. confirmatur eorum testimonio qui artem memoriae tradiderunt.
Ass. ib. Now that hath the verse in effect.
Con. ib. Now that verse far exceedeth.

Praeterea poeticae dimensionis utilitas ad juvandam memoriam demonstratur effecto & subjecto. effectum concluditur enthymemate:

Poetarum nonnulla carmina percepta in flore adolescentiae usque ad senectutem memoria custodiuntur.
Ergo poetica dimensio confert memoriae.

Subjectum[20] etiam judicatur enthymemate.

Artium variarum praecepta ut grammaticae, logicae, mathematicae sunt tradita carminibus.
Dimensio igitur poetica valet ad juvandam memoriam.

|f. 25ᵛ| *Secunda* calumnia qualis est? tali syllogismo concluditur.

Si aliae sint artes meliores poesi & in quibus opera nostra melius ponitur poesis vituperanda est.
At aliae sunt artes meliores poesi etc.
Ergo poesis est vituperanda.

Hujus calumniae syllogismum refellis dum & propositionis consequentiam negas & convincis assumptionem falsitatis.

Consequentiae negatio. ib. And certaynly though.

finitie to memory) beeing so set as one word cannot be lost but the whole worke failes" (183).

Assumption: "be it in ryme or measured verse, by the former a man shall haue a neere gesse to the follower" (183).

Conclusion: "Now, that Verse farre exceedeth Prose" (182).

Next this same Assumption, already illustrated through a comparison from the lesser and through definition, is explained further, now from helping causes,[51] concluded in a full syllogism of the second figure:

> Keeping distinct the seats and places of argument greatly strengthens memory.
> In verse the seats and places are kept distinct.
> Verse therefore greatly strengthens memory.

Proposition: "lastly, euen they that haue taught the Art of memory haue shewed nothing so apt for it as a certaine roome deuided into many places well and throughly knowne" (183). It is confirmed by the testimony of those who have taught the art of memory.

Assumption: "Now, that hath the verse in effect perfectly, euery word hauing his naturall seate, which seate must needes make the words remembred" (183).

Conclusion: "Now, that Verse farre exceedeth Prose" (182).

> Next the usefulness of verse in aiding memory is shown from effect and from subject. The effect is set out in an enthymeme:
>> Some songs of the poets, learned in the flower of youth, stay in memory even to old age.
>> Thus verse aids memory.
> The subject is also disposed in an enthymeme:
>> The precepts of different arts, such as grammar, logic, and mathematics, have been taught in poems.
>> Verse, therefore, has the power to aid memory.

The second calumny: Of what sort is it? It is outlined in the following syllogism:

> If other arts are better than poetry, and if our efforts are better directed to them, then poetry is to be censured.
> But other arts are better than poetry, etc.
> Therefore, poetry is to be censured.

You argue against the syllogism of this calumny both when you deny the consequent of the Proposition, and when you show the falseness of the syllogism's Assumption.

Negation of the consequent: "And certainly, though a man should graunt their first assumption, it should followe (me thinkes) very

Assumptio refellitur ab effectis poeseos.
>Quae disciplina & tradit virtutem hominibus & animum amore
>ejusdem accendit, ea est optima.
>At poesis & tradit hominibus virtutem & animum ejusdem amore
>accendit.
>Poesis igitur est optima.

Prop. ib. for yf it be as J affirme.
Ass. ib. And that none can both.
Con. ib. Then is ye conclusion. & ib. But J still & utterly.

Sequitur[21] tertia *Calumnia*.
>*Poesis* est mendaciorum parens:
>ac proinde reprehendenda.

Antecedenti respondes primum e Comparatione: quod scilicet ex omnibus artibus poesis sit minime mendax. comparationis demonstratio
est ab adjuvante causa mendacii:
>Astronomia, geometria, medicina, caeteraeque artes affirmant
>cum poeta nihil affirmet.
>Itaque facilius mentiuntur quam poeta.

Anteced. ib. And no lesse of the rest.
Conseq. ib. The Astronomer wth his. |f. 26|
Est etiam enthymematis pars utraque in unum enuntiatum comprehen-
sa. ib. So as the other artists.

Deinde antecedenti parti Calumniae respondetur e Contradictione:
quod scilicet poesis non omnino mentiatur. ad contradictionis illustrationem affertur definitio conclusa syll. expl. prim. spe.
>Mentiri est affirmare id esse verum quod falsum est.
>Poesis nihil affirmat.
>Poesis itaque non mentitur.

vnwillingly, that good is not good because better is better" (184).
The Assumption is refuted from poetry's effects:

> That discipline is best that both teaches men and inflames the mind
> with the love of virtue.
> But poetry teaches men virtue and inflames the mind with the
> love of virtue.
> Thus poetry is best.

Proposition: "for if it be, as I affirme, that no learning is so good as
that which teacheth and mooueth to vertue" (184).

Assumption: "and that none can both teach and moue thereto so much
as Poetry: (184).

Conclusion: "then is the conclusion manifest that Incke and Paper cannot be to a more profitable purpose employed" (184), and "But I
still and vtterly denye that there is sprong out of earth a more
fruitefull knowledge" (184).

The third calumny follows:

> Poetry is the parent of lies,
> And is therefore to be censured.

You first answer the Antecedent of this enthymeme from a
comparison — surely, that of all the arts, poetry lies least. The
demonstration of this comparison is developed through the helping
cause of lying:

> Astronomy, Geometry, Medicine, and the other arts affirm things,
> while the poet affirms nothing.
> They, therefore, lie more readily than the poet.

Antecedent: "And no lesse of the rest, which take vpon them to affirme" (184).

Consequent: "The Astronomer, with his cosen the Geometrician, can
hardly escape, when they take vpon them to measure the height of
the starres" (184).

Both parts of this enthymeme are also included in a single axiom: "So
as the other Artists, and especially the Historian, affirming many
things, can, in the cloudy knowledge of mankinde, hardly escape
from many lyes" (184).

Then, to the Antecedent of the calumny you respond from contradiction, arguing, or course, that poetry does not lie at all. To illustrate
this contradiction you give a definition, set out in a full syllogism
of the first figure:

> To lie is to affirm something to be true that is false.
> Poetry affirms nothing.
> Poetry therefore does not lie.

Prop. ib. To lye is to affirme.

Ass. ib. Now for the poet.

Conc. ib. Therefore never lyeth.

Propositio non est καθόλου πρῶτον. Nam & is mentitur qui negat id
esse verum, quod reipsa verum est: ut si quis hoc modo enuntiet
sensa mentis, *Homo non est animal*. In hoc axiomate non affirmo id
esse verum, quod falsum est. at dices fortasse, fateri ⌜te⌝ esse axioma negatum idque falsum: non tamen mentiri, si quis mente con-
sentanea argumenta negando sic enuntiet, nisi insuper affirmet nova
actione mentis, id est, alio enuntiato hoc falsum enuntiatum esse
verum. Ne sic quidem liberas a culpa propositionem syllogismi.
AEque enim mentitur qui affirmat id esse falsum, quod verum est,
quam qui affirm[at] id esse verum quod falsum est: ut si affirmen
hoc enuntiatum, *Homo est animal*, esse falsum. Deinde mendacium
metiri non e dispositione argumentorum, qua enuntiatur uti res est
aut non est, non est id logicae doctrinae praeceptis de veritate &
falsitate satis consentaneum. ut verum enuntiatum id est, quando
pronuntiat, uti rei natura fert: sic illud falsum erit & mendax ax-
ioma, quando a rei natura alienum quid enuntiat, etiamsi |f. 26ᵛ|
mentis affirmatio non accesserit: quae hercle quid aliud est quam
argumentum testimonii, quo aut verum enuntiatum asseritur esse
falsum aut falsum esse verum. Porro si mendacium non existat, nisi
affirmatione nostra, id est, argumento testimonii asseratur sententiam veram esse falsam aut falsam esse veram: profecto veritas non
existet, si ad alterius enuntiati sententiam probandam vel improban-
dam mentis assensum & testimonium non attuleris. At veritas ex
isto assensu & testimonio non pendet, sed e rerum natura & dispositione oritur: adeo ut etiamsi adventitium illud defuerit, nihilominus
veritatis essentia constare possit.

Quod ad Assumptionem attinet, est illa quidem vera, si non de affirmatione, quae ex argumenti cum argumento velut amica compositione nascitur intelligatur: sed de illa, quae testimonii vim habet ad
alterius enuntiati explicationem. Sin vero speciem affirmationis
priorem notas, poesis est in affirmatione axiomatum frequens.

Proposition: "to lye is to affirme that to be true which is false" (184).
Assumption: "Now, for the Poet, he nothing affirmes" (184).
Conclusion: "therefore neuer lyeth" (184).

Your Proposition here fails to deal with the most general level of argument.[52] For one who lies denies that something is true which is in
fact true, as if someone were to express a thought in this way: *Man
is not an animal.* In this axiom, I do not "affirm" that something which
is false is true. But you will perhaps reply that you agree this axiom
has been negated and is false, but nevertheless that it is not lying
if someone makes a statement in this way, negating arguments that
(as it were) agree with each other in his mind, unless he should affirm through a new mental act, i.e., a further statement, that this
false axiom is true. But surely you cannot free the Proposition of
your syllogism from blame that way. Anyone who affirms something
to be false which is true lies equally as much as one who affirms
something to be true which is false; as if I were to affirm that the
axiom *Man is an animal* is false. Not to judge a lie through the disposition of the arguments by which it is claimed that something does
or does not exist is not sufficiently in accord with the precepts of
logic dealing with truth and falsity. Just as an axiom is true when
it states how the nature of the matter stands, similarly, that axiom
will be false and lying when it states something that does not agree
with the nature of the matter, even if an affirmation of the mind
is not added on. And indeed what is that further affirmation, to be
sure, other than an argument drawn from testimony, in which either
a true axiom is said to be false, or a false axiom is said to be true?
Finally, if there is no lie except by our affirmation, unless, that is,
it is asserted in an argument from testimony that a true statement
is false, or a false one true, than certainly truth will not exist, if you
do not bring both mental assent and testimony to proving or disproving the sense of this further statement. But truth does not depend
upon this mental assent and testimony; instead it arises from the
nature of things and from disposition. This is true to such an extent
that even if that adventitious argument from testimony is lacking,
the essence of truth can still be established.

As for what pertains to your Assumption ["Now, for the Poet, he
nothing affirmes"], that is certainly true, if we are thinking not of
an affirmation that arises from the amicable assembling, as it were,
of one argument with another, but rather of that affirmation that
has the force of testimony to making that further truth-claim. But
if you consider that first kind of affirmation, poetry is rich in the
affirmation of axioms.

Porro calumniae occuritur ab adjuncta qualitate Mendacis:
  Mendax est qui vult illis fidem haberi, quae ab ipso proferuntur.
  Poeta non vult illis fidem haberi quae ab ipso proferuntur.
  Poeta igitur non est mendax.
Prop. deest.
Ass. ib. The poet never.
Con. ib. And therfore though.

Denique refutatur calumnia e definitione poeseos.
  Allegorica fictio rei quae esse aut non esse debeat non mentitur.
  Poesis est hujusmodi allegorica fictio.
  Poesis itaque non mentitur. |f. 27|
Prop. ib. They will never.
Ass. ib. yf then a man.
Con. ib. so in poesy. arguitur e simili.

Propositio confirmatur e speciebus.
  si allegorica fictio mentitur, Nathanis oratio ad Davidem, fabula
    AEsopi, inscriptio Thebarum in foribus mentitur.
  At hoc falsum est.
  itaque & illud.
Prop. ib. w^thout wee will say. propositio suis partibus integra non
  exprimitur.
Ass. ib. W^ch as a wicked man durst.
Con. ib. They will never give.

Hîc adversus assumptionem illam, quae a poeta removet adjunctam
  qualitatem mendacis, objicitur poetam de proponenda veritate
  cogitare, quia nomina imponit iis, de quibus scribit. istud diluitur
  & e pari & e fine.
  E pari. Nec jureconsultus nomina ficta imponens cum tractat
    causam, nec is qui fictitias appellationes tessellis accommodat,
    mentitur. Jtaque nec poeta.

  E fine. Poeta imponit nomina adcirco, ut imago illa, quam pingit,

Next the calumny is attacked from the adjunct of the liar's nature:
  A liar is someone who wants the things he writes to be believed.
  The poet does not want the things he writes to be believed.
  The poet is therefore not a liar.
Proposition: omitted.
Assumption: "The Poet neuer maketh any circles about your imagina-
  tion, to coniure you to beleeue for true what he writes" (185).
Conclusion: "and therefore, though he recount things not true, yet
  because hee telleth them not for true, he lyeth not" (185).

Finally the calumny is refuted from the definition of poetry:
  An allegorical fiction of something that either should or should
    not be, does not lie.
  Poetry is this kind of allegorical fiction.
  Poetry, therefore, does not lie.
Proposition: "they will neuer giue the lye to things not affirmatiuely
  but allegorically and figuratiuely written" (185).
Assumption: "If then a man can ariue, at that childs age, to know that
  the Poets persons and dooings are but pictures what should be" (185).
Conclusion: "so in Poesie, looking for fiction, they shal vse the narra-
  tion but as an imaginatiue groundplot of a profitable inuention"
  (185). This is argued by simile.

The Proposition is confirmed from species:
  If allegory lies, then Nathan's speech to David, Aesop's fables, the
    inscription "Thebes" over doors all lie.
  But this is false.
  Therefore the rest is false too.
Proposition: "without we will say that *Nathan* lyed in his speech" (185).
  The whole Proposition is not set out in its parts.
Assumption: "Which as a wicked man durst scarce say, so think I none
  so simple would say that *Esope* lyed in the tales of his beasts" (185).
Conclusion: "they will neuer giue the lye to things not affirmatiuely
  but allegorically and figuratiuely written" (185).

Here, against the earlier Assumption that the poet does not have the
qualities of a liar, it is objected that the poet intends to deal with
truth, because he gives names to the people he writes about. This
objection is answered both from a comparison of equals, and from
the final cause.
  From the equal: the lawyer does not lie in using false names when
    he argues a case, nor does anyone who applies false names to
    chessmen. Neither, then, does the poet.
  From the final cause: the poet gives names in order that the image

videri posset illustrior: ut ostendat quid homines hujus aut il-
lius conditionis oporteat agere. |f. 27^v|

Quarta calumnia est de abusu.
  Poesis abutitur hominum ingeniis alliciens ea ad lasciviam &
  amorem.
  Vituperanda igitur.

Negas antecedentem sed praemissa apostrophe ad amorem. negatio
est e Diversis:
  Non poesis abutitur hominis ingenio, sed hominis ingenium
  abutitur poesi.

Licentiam hanc contendi poetica facultate declaras e Similibus:
  Protas. ib. as the Paynter.
  Apod. ib. for J wil not deny.
Jam vero siquis hoc modo concludat:
  Hominis ingenium abutitur poesi:
  ideoque[22] poesis vituperanda est.
Tu vitiosam consequentiam esse doces: immo eo argumento laudem
non labem poeseos concludi posse:
  Abusus poeticae facultatis maxime obest.
  itaque legitimus usus maxime prodest.
Deinde vitium consequentiae notas e paribus:
  Abusus medicinae, jurisprudentiae, verbi divini, acus, gladii non
  facit ut hae res jure vituperentur.
  itaque nec abusus poeseos facit ut poesis merito reprehendatur.

Quinta calumnia talis est.
  Poesis traduxit Britannorum animos ab actione rerum ad theorias.
  Poesis igitur vituperanda est. |f. 28|
Antecedentem calumniatores hoc modo confirmant:
  Priscis ante poetas temporibus homines sese ad agendum non ad
  contemplandum retulerunt.
  Jtaque cum exortis poetis sese ab actione ad contemplationem
  sevocaverint, factum est id poetarum culpa.

he paints can seem more clear, so that he can show what men should do in this or that situation.

The fourth calumny concerns abuse.
   Poetry abuses men's wits, drawing them to lasciviousness and love.
   It is therefore to be censured.

After an apostrophe to love, you deny the first term of this enthymeme.
   The denial is from differences:
   Poetry does not abuse man's wit; rather, man's wit abuses poetry.

From a comparison of likes you explain that such licentiousness has indeed been brought about through poetry:
   Protasis: "As the Painter, that shoulde giue to the eye eyther some excellent perspectiue, or some fine picture. . .may leaue those, and please an ill-pleased eye with wanton shewes of better hidden matters" (186–87).
   Apodosis: "For I will not denie but that mans wit may make Poesie (which should be *Eikastike*, which some learned haue defined, figuring foorth good things) to be *Phantastike*: which doth, contrariwise, infect the fancie with vnworthy obiects" (186).
But now someone might argue like this:
   Man's wit abuses poetry.
   Therefore poetry is to be censured.
You explain that the consequent of this argument is wrong; on the contrary, from this argument one can praise poetry, not disgrace it.
   The abuse of poetry does the most harm.
   Therefore the right use does the most good.
Then you describe the error of this argument's consequence through a comparison of equals:
   The abuse of medicine, of law, of the word of God, of a needle, of a sword, does not rightly allow these things to be condemned.
   Neither, then, should the abuse of poetry rightly allow it to be condemned.

The fifth calumny is of the following sort:
   Poetry drew the minds of the English from doing things to theorizing.
   Poetry is therefore to be condemned.
Critics support the first term of this enthymeme like this:
   In earlier times, before poets, men gave themselves to action, not to contemplation.
   Thus when poets had sprung up and men withdrew themselves from action in favor of contemplation, it was the poets' fault.

Hujus posterioris enthymematis consecutio refellitur dum negatur
fuisse tempus illud, cum nulli in Britannia Poetae existerent.

Prioris enthymematis antecedentem elevas a paribus: quia idem potest
objici aeque adversus caeteras artes ac poesin: ut constat Gothi cujusdam testimonio.

Verum non modo a paribus sed etiam a subjecto disputas adversus
antecedentem.

  Poesis est gratussima comes militum in Campo & acie.
  Quî igitur traducit ab actione?
Antecedens explicatur e specie.
  Orlandus furiosus & Arthurus erunt militibus grati.
  Orlandus furiosus & Arthurus sunt poesei.
  Poesis igitur erit grata militibus.
Propositio amplificatur e Dissimilibus. Theoriae illi jejunae de Ente
& prima materia non convenit cum thorace perinde ut Orlando
furioso.

Conclusio exaggeratur effecto duplici: nempe & quod poesis delectationem afferat Turcis ac Tartaris: & quod in Graecis primo pepererit
animi magnitudinem.

Hoc posterius effectum arguitur primo e Simili:
  protas. ib. Truly it may seeme.
  Apod. ib. So theyr active men. |f. 28ᵛ|
Deinde e pari.

  Si Alexander animi magnitudinem a poetis accepit, probabile est
  & caeteros Graecos eandem a poetis accepisse.
  At Alexander a poetis animi magnitudinem accepit.
  itaque & caeteri Graeci.

Prop. ib. Only Alexanders example: quasi diceretur quod Alexandro
contigit, idem caeteris contigisse probabile esse.

Ass. ib. This Alexander leaft his.

Con. ib. So theyr active men.

Ad Assumptionis exornationem laudatur Alexander e testimonio
Plutarchi, ex effectis, e simili, quod nempe sit phaenix e dissimilibus.

Sequitur duplex prolepsis adversus poetas. prior adversus poetam En-
nium e M. Catonis authoritate & facto. Ad Catonis authoritatem

The logical force of this enthymeme is undermined when one denies that there was ever a time when there were no poets in Britain.

You attack the Antecedent of the first enthymeme from a comparison of equals, since the same objection can equally be made against other arts as against poetry, as is clear from the testimony of a certain Goth.

Indeed, you argue against this Antecedent not just from equals, but also from poetry's subject:

> Poetry is a most welcome companion among soldiers, both in camp and in battle.
>
> How then does it discourage action?

The first term of this argument is developed from species:

> *Orlando Furioso* and *Arthur* will be welcome among soldiers.
> *Orlando Furioso* and *Arthur* are poems.
> Poetry will thus be welcome among soldiers.

The Proposition is amplified from a comparison of unlikes. Those empty theories of *Ens* and *Prima Materia* do not agree with a corselet, just as they do not agree with *Orlando Furioso*.

The Conclusion is expanded further through two effects: namely, both that poetry should bring delight to Turks and Tartars, and that it was the first to bring about great courage among the Greeks.

This last effect is argued first in a simile:

> Protasis: "truly it may seeme, that as by him [i.e.., Homer] their learned men tooke almost their first light of knowledge" (188–89).
>
> Apodosis: "so their actiue men receiued their first motions of courage" (189).

Then from equals:

> If Alexander took great courage from poets, it is likely that the rest of the Greeks took the same from poets.
> But Alexander did take great courage from poets.
> Thus the rest of the Greeks as well.

Proposition: "Onlie *Alexanders* example may serue" (189), as if to have suggested that whatever affected Alexander, the same thing probably affected the rest.

Assumption: "This *Alexander* left his Schoolemaister, liuing *Aristotle*, behind him, but tooke dead *Homer* with him" (189).

Conclusion: "so their actiue men receiued their first motions of courage" (189)

To embellish the Assumption, Alexander is praised from Plutarch's testimony, from effects, from simile (that indeed he is a Phoenix of warlike princes), and from unlikes.

You then anticipate two objections against poets, the first of which, from the authority and practice of Marcus Cato, is against the poet

elevandam Cato describitur triplici argumento e Diversis. Deinde
prolepsi occuritur partim e Diversorum distinctione. Non poesis Ennii sed persona Ennii est improbata a Catone: partim e praestan-
tium hominum majore authoritate & facto nempe Fulvii, Nasicae,
Scipionis Asiatici & Africani.
posterior prolepsis est e Platonis authoritate.
 primo refellitur prolepsis e paribus. paria enim objiciuntur contra Platonem caeterosque philosophos.
 Deinde prolepsis elevatur e subjecto loco, unde ejecti sunt poetae:
 nempe e rep. in qua uxorum communitas est approbata.
 Tum e Diversis: Plato abusum poeseos non poesin reprehendit.
 quod declaratur e similibus:
  Protas. ib. Saynt Paule.
  Apod. ib. So doth Plato. |f. 29|
 Verum non modo e similibus ostenditur, sed etiam e specie con-
 cluditur Platonem reprehendisse abusum poeseos.
 Inductio falsarum de Deo opinionum a poetis est abusus poeseos.
 Plato reprehendit inductionem istam.
 Plato igitur abusum poeseos reprehendit.
Prop. omit.
Ass. ib. Plato found fault. & ib. Plato therfore whose.
Con. ib. So as Plato banishing.

Assumptio amplificatur e fine reprehensae inductionis: ne juventus
 scilicet imbueretur falsis de Deo opinionibus.
 Quod vero affirmet Plato inductas fuisse has opiniones a poetis,
 in eo Platoni e Diversis resistitur:
  Poetae non induxerunt has opiniones, sed inductas ab aliis
  imitatione expresserunt: ut constat e testimonio historiae.

Ennius. To attack Cato's authority, you describe him in a three-fold argument from differences. Then you answer the objection partly from a distinction drawn between these differences (it is not the poetry but the person of Ennius that Cato disapproved), and partly from the greater authority and practice of outstanding men like Fulvius, Nasica, the Scipios of Asia and of Africa.

The second objection is from the authority of Plato.

> First this objection is answered from a comparison of equals: the same complaints are made against Plato and the rest of the philosophers.
>
> Then the objection is attacked from the subject of the place from which the poets have been ejected — namely, from the Republic, where holding wives in common was approved.
>
> Then from an argument of differences: Plato criticizes the abuse of poetry, not poetry itself. This is argued from a comparison of likes:
>
>> Protasis: "S. *Paule* himselfe, who (yet for credite of Poets) alledgeth twise two Poets, and one of them by the name of a Prophet, setteth a watch-word vpon Philosophy" (191).
>>
>> Apodisis: "So dooth *Plato* vpon the abuse, not vpon Poetrie" (191).
>
> Indeed, not only do you show from a comparison of likes that Plato was criticizing the abuse of poetry, and not poetry itself, but you also conclude the same by an argument from species:
>
> For poets to induce false opinions of God is an abuse of poetry.
> Plato criticized this sort of induction.
> Plato thus criticized the abuse of poetry.

Proposition: omitted.

Assumption: "*Plato* found fault that the Poets of his time filled the worlde with wrong opinions of the Gods" (191), and "*Plato* therefore (whose authoritie I had much rather iustly conster then vniustly resist) meant not in general of Poets." (191).

Conclusion: "So as *Plato*, banishing the abuse, not the thing, not banishing it, but giuing due honor vnto it, shall be our Patron and not our aduersarie" (192).

This Assumption is amplified from the final cause of his having criticized this induction: surely that youth should not have been imbued with false opinions about God.

> Where Plato claims that poets induced these opinions, you answer him from an argument of differences:
>
>> Poets did not induce these opinons, but expressed through imitation opinions induced by others; as is clear from the testimony of Greek story.

Postremo non poesin sed abusum poeseos a Platone reprehensum esse patet ex effecto Platonis: qui effert in Dialogo quodam poesin divinis laudibus. Effectum istud augetur e simili facto Alexandri, Caesaris, Scipionum, Laelii, Socratis, Aristotelis, Plutarchi. Ex hiis posteriores quatuor laudantur ab effectis.

Hactenus multiplex prolepsis adversus poetas refutata est. Ἀνακεφαλαίωσις continet laudem poetae ex adjuncto ornamento laureae.

Quid jam sequitur? certe prolepsis de poetarum contemptu apud Anglos. cui respondetur e causis,[23] quibus Anglia adducetur ut poesin rejiciat & aspernetur. Antequam de causis disputas tuam de hujusmodi contemptu admirationem amplificas:

Primo ab adjuncto Angliae: quia est parens excellentium ingeniorum, ideoque nullam causam subesse cur poetas, qui vincunt caeteros divinitate ingenii, aspernetur. |f. 29ᵛ|

Tum e comparatione parium.

Poesis & culta est & jam colitur in aliis nationibus a regibus, senatoribus, ducibus, oratoribus. ib. Sweet poesy.

Cur igitur in Anglia ab Anglis non coleretur? ib. That poesy.

Deinde e [fic]to Minori.

Ipsa terra poeseos in Anglia contemptum deflet, ut apparet ex effecto terrae comprehenso in enuntiatum a Majore. Terra nunc parit lauros multo quam solebat pauciores.

Quis igitur non mirabitur rejectam in Anglia poesin?

Post e paribus.

Floruerunt olim in Angliae poetae.

Cur igitur jam non florent?

Protasis arguitur ex adjuncto tempore. Floruerunt belli tempore.

& e Dissimili: at nunc contemnuntur: ubi ad contemptum illustrandum adhibetur comparatio parium. ib. They ar almost in as good.

Admirationis tuae amplificatio ejusmodi est. sequitur causarum explicatio.

Finally, that Plato criticized not poetry but the abuse of poetry is evident from the effect of Plato, who in a certain dialogue exalts poetry with divine praises. You embellish this effect by citing similar praise by Alexander, Caesar, the Scipios, Lelius, Socrates, Aristotle, Plutarch. Of these, the last four are praised from effects.

At this point the multiple objection against poets has been answered. Your recapitulation contains praise of the poet from the adjunct of his being decorated with laurels.

What comes next? Clearly you anticipate an objection concerning the contempt of poetry among the English. You answer this objection from the causes that lead England to reject and scorn poetry. Before you discuss these causes, you amplify your amazement at such contempt.

First from an adjunct of England: since England is the parent of excellent wits, there is no cause for England to scorn poets, who surpass all others in divinity of wit.

Then from a comparison of equals:

Poetry has been cultivated, and is still cultivated, in other nations by kings, senators, leaders, orators: "Sweete Poesie, that hath aunciently had Kings, Emperors, Senators, great Captaines" (193).

So why is it not cultivated in England by the English? "That Poesie, thus embraced in all other places, should onely finde in our time a hard welcome in England" (194).

Then from a feigned comparison from the lesser:[53]

The earth itself bewails the contempt of poetry in England, as is clear from the earth's effect, as given in an argument from a comparison from the greater: the earth now bears fewer laurels than it once did.

Who, therefore, will not be amazed that poetry has been rejected in England?

After that, from a comparison of equals:

Poets once flourished in England.

So why do they not flourish now?

The first term is argued from the adjunct of time: they flourished in the time of war. And from unlikeness: but now they are condemned; where to illustrate this condemnation, you use a comparison of equals: "they are almost in as good reputation as the *Mountibancks* at *Venice*" (194).

That is how you amplify your amazement. Now follows an explanation of causes.

Contemptus duplicem causam facis alteram e subjecto poeseos: ab Anglorum adjunctis alteram.

Illa e subjecto concluditur enthymemate.

Angli fugiunt Martem. ib. wch now can scarce.

Quid ergo miri est si fugiant poesin? ib. So it serves for.

Enthymematis consecutio pendet e comparatione Majorum. Poesis multo malit illigari cum Marte in rete quam frui domestico otio: quod declaratur e simili sed interposita notatione diversi finis.

Illa ab adjunctis causa est *inscitia* tractandae poeseos in iis qui in excudendis poematis versantur.

Jam vero contemni poesin propter artificum in texendo poemate singularem imperitiam docetur e Similibus.

Protas. ib. And so as Epaminundas.

Apod. ib. So there men. |f. 30|

Apodosis similium explicatur e deformatae poeseos efficiente, nempe publicatione poematum refr^{r}a^{l}gantibus Musis.

Publicatio poematum ⟨tractatur⟩ reprehenditur & ab effecto & e Dissimili.

Publicationis effectum est mirifica defatigatio legentium: quae amplificatur e Minoribus. ib. more weary.

Dissimil. Homines excellenti ingenio & judicio continent se a scribendo.

At hii quibus nullus est genius, ad id se referunt.

Prot. ib. while in the meane tyme. ubi est comparatio Majorum.

Apod. ib. for now as yf. & ib. uppon this necessarily.

You establish two causes of contempt, the first taken from the subject of poetry, the second from adjuncts of the English.
The cause argued from subject is set out in an enthymeme:
   The English flee from Mars: "which nowe can scarce endure the payne of a pen." (194).
   Why, then, should it be surprising if they flee from poetry? "so serues it for a peece of a reason why they are lesse gratefull to idle England" (194).
   The logical force of this enthymeme depends upon a comparison from the greater: poetry much prefers being caught in the net with Mars to enjoying homely quiet. That is argued from likeness, but with the observation concerning its different object inserted ["which like *Venus* (but to better purpose)" (194)].

The cause argued from adjuncts is the ignorance in dealing with poetry among those who are busy forging poems.
Now in fact you explain from a comparison of likes that poetry is condemned for the singular awkwardness of these poets in making poems.
   Protasis: "And so, as *Epaminondas* is sayd, with the honor of his vertue, to haue made an office, by his exercising it, which before was contemptible, to become highly respected" (194).
   Apodosis: "so these, no more but setting their names to it, by their owne disgracefulnes disgrace the most gracefull Poesie" (194).
The second term of this simile is explained from the efficient cause of how poetry has been deformed, i.e., by the publication of poems disgraceful to the Muses.
   This publication of poems is criticized both from effect, and from unlikeness.
   The effect of publication is an extraordinary weariness of readers; this is amplified from a comparison from the lesser: "more weary then Post-horses" (194).
   From unlikeness: Outstanding men of wit and judgment keep themselves from writing, but those who have no wit apply themselves to it.
   Protasis: "while, in the mean tyme, they *Queis meliore luto finxit praecordia Titan*, are better content to suppresse the out-flowing of their wit" (194–95), where the comparison is from the greater.
   Apodosis: "For now, as if all the Muses were gotte with childe, to bring foorth bastard Poets, without any commission they doe poste ouer the banckes of *Helicon*" (194), and "Vpon this necessarily followeth, that base men with seruile wits vndertake it" (194).

Sedenim quae causa est hujus in tractando poemate inscitiae & in-
solentiae? Hîc tu duplicem efficientem notas hujus inscitiae, nempe
defectum & nativi genii & diligentis culturae. utraque efficiens est
conclusa syl. exp. pri. sp.
   Poematis texendi facultas oritur e genio & cultura genii, id est,
   arte, imitatione, exercitatione scienter adhibita.
   Angli illi, a quibus cuduntur poemata non habent genium, non
   culturam genii perite adhibent.
   Angli igitur non habent poematis texendi facultatem.

Propositionis pars de genio. ib. A poet noe industrie. tractatur diversis testimonio duplici, dissimili. Propositionis pars de cultura genii.
ib. So must the hiestflying. habet exornationem e simili.
Assumptionis pars de genio. ib. Taking uppon us to be. de cultura
genii non adhibita perite. ib. But these nether artificiall.
   Adhibitae culturae imperitia demonstratur & e subjectis & ex ef-
   fecto. |f. 30v|
Subjecta concluduntur enthymemate:
   Nec in rebus nec in verbis cultura illa perite adhibita est.
   itaque non omnino perite adhibita est.

   Effectum imperitiae judicatur etiam enthymemate.
   Rem confuse & perturbate tractant.
   Non igitur perite versantur in adhibenda cultura.

Adversus utriusque enthymematis antecedentem objici potest perfec-
ta poemata esse Chawseri Troilum, speculum Magistratuum, Odas
Surriensis, Pastoris Calendarium, Gorboducam. Sed objectio ista
occupata est e Diversis. quasi diceres, Etsi valde laudabilia poemata
sunt, tamen offendunt tractationis nonnulla imperitia.
In quibus offensum sit a Pastoris Calendario & Gorboduca ostendis.

But what actually is the cause of this ignorance and ineptness in writing poems? Here you mention two efficient causes of ignorance, namely, a defect both in native genius and in diligent practice. The two causes are dealt with in a full syllogism of the first figure:

> The ability to write poems begins with genius and the training of genius, which is to say, with art, imitation, and practice, expertly applied.
>
> These Englishmen by whom poems are forged do not have genius, nor do they make skillful use of the training of genius.
>
> The English, therefore, do not have the ability to write poetry.

Proposition: the part concerning genius: "A Poet no industrie can make, if his owne *Genius* bee not carried vnto it" (195). It is dealt with from differences, in a doubled testimony of unlikes [i.e., *"Orator fit; Poeta nascitur"* (195)]. The part of the Proposition that concerns the training of genius is embellished from likeness: "[as the firtilest ground must bee manured,] so must the highest flying wit haue a *Dedalus* to guide him" (195).

Assumption: the part concerning genius: "taking vpon vs to be Poets in despight of *Pallas*" (195). The part concerning the training of genius that is unskillfully used: "But these, neyther artificiall rules nor imitatiue patternes, we much cumber our selues withall" (195).

> The unskillfulness in their use of training is shown both from subjects and from effect.

> The subjects are set out in an enthymeme:
>
>> Neither in matter nor in words has this training been skillfully used.
>>
>> Therefore it has not at all been skillfully used.

> The effect of this lack of skill is also disposed in an enthymeme:
>
>> They deal with things confusedly and obscurely.
>>
>> They are therefore not making use of their training skillfully.

Against the first term of each enthymeme it can be objected that Chaucer's *Troilus*, the *Mirror of Magistrates*, Surrey's *Odes*, *The Shepheardes Calender*, and *Gorboduc* are perfect poems. But you have anticipated this objection in an argument from differences: it is as if you were to say, even if these poems are very much to be praised, they still err through some ineptness in their handling.

You show how *The Shepheardes Calender* and *Gorboduc* offend. The first poem errs in the adjunct of language, the second in the adjuncts of its circumstances. The kind of language is criticized from its unlikeness to the practice of Theocrites, Virgil, Sanazarro.

That *Gorboduc* errs in its circumstances is shown both from differences

illud poema in adjuncto idiomate, hoc in adjunctis circumstantiis
peccat. idiomatis genus reprehenditur e Dissimili facto Theocriti,
Virgili, Sanazarae.
Peccare Gorboducam in circumstantiis ostenditur & e Diversis. ib. w^ch
not w^thstanding. & e speciebus conclusis enthym.
Peccat loco & tempori. ib. for it is faulty.
Peccat igitur circumstantiis. ib. yet in troth it.
Antecedens confirmatur adjuncto Gorboducae, nempe repraesenta-
tione plurium locorum & dierum.
Tragaedia libera ab offensione loci & temporis repraesentare debet
unum locum unumque diem.
Gorboduca non repraesentat unum duntaxat locum unumque
diem.
Gorboduca igitur non est immunis ab offensione loci & temporis.
|f. 31| Prop. ib. for where the stage. probatur testimonio Aristotelis.
Ass. ib. there is both many dayes.
Con. ib. for it is faulty.

Constat jam ab hiis principibus poematum authoribus offensum esse.
Aliorum in hoc genere offensionem concludis e Majoribus:
Gorboduca offendit in rebus tractatis.
Multo igitur magis offendunt poemata aliorum.

Enthymematis consequens demonstratur ab adjuncta repraesentatione
variorum locorum & temporum.
A quibus fabulis varii loci & varia tempora repraesentantur, eae
adversus communem sensum, antiquum morem, Italicam con-
suetudinem offendunt.
At nostrorum hominum fabulae varios locos & tempora
repraesentant.
itaque vehementer offendunt.

Prop. ib. wch how absurd.
Ass. ib. where yow shall.
Con. ib. How much more.
Prolepsis est adversus propositionem de Eunucho Terentii: cui oc-
curitur ab efficiente nempe fabulae actione diversa in duos dies.

("which notwithstanding, as it is full of stately speeches and well sounding Phrases. . .yet in troth it is very defectious in the circumstances" [196-97]) and from species, set out in an enthymeme:

It errs in place and time: "For it is faulty both in place and time, the two necessary companions of all corporall actions" (197).

Thus it errs in circumstances: "yet in troth it is very defective in the circumstances" (197).

The Antecedent is confirmed through an adjunct of *Gorboduc*, namely, its representing many places and days.

A tragedy that does not offend in place and time ought to represent one place and one day.

Gorboduc does not represent just one place and one day.

Gorboduc thus offends in place and time.

Proposition: "For where the stage should alwaies represent but one place, and the vttermost time presupposed in it should be, both by *Aristotles* precept and common reason, but one day" (197). This is argued from the testimony of Aristotle.

Assumption: "there is both many dayes, and many places, inartificially imagined" (197).

Conclusion: "For it is faulty both in place and time" (197).

You have now established through these leading writers of poetry that an offense exists. In a comparison from the greater, you now show that other writers offend in the same way:

Gorboduc offends in its treatment of things.

Therefore, the poems of others offend much more.

The second term of this enthymeme is demonstrated from the adjunct of the representation of various places and times.

Those by whom various places and times are represented in plays offend against common sense, ancient custom, and the Italian tradition.

But our writers' plays represent various places and times.

Thus they offend greatly.

Proposition: "which how absurd it is in sence euen sence may imagine, and Arte hath taught, and all auncient examples iustified, and, at this day, the ordinary Players in Italie wil not erre in" (197).

Assumption: "where you shal haue *Asia* of the one side, and *Affrick* of the other (197).

Conclusion: "[But if it be so in *Gorboduck*,] how much more in al the rest?" (197).

There is against your Proposition a possible objection concerning Terence's *Eunuch*; it is answered with the efficient cause, that

De Plauti errore confiteris: cum tamen extenuas ab adjuncto, quod
sit unicus.
Est & alia prolepsis de difficultate historiae explicandae varios locos
& tempora complexae. sed refutatur e Diversis:
Tragaedia non est astricta legibus historiae sed poeseos.
Locorum & temporum varietas est narranda non actu
repraesentanda.
Non est ordiendum ab ovo sed a principe parte illius actionis quae
repraesentanda est. rem propositam exemplo illustras.|f. 31ᵛ|

Reprehensis[25] nostrorum hominum fabulis propter adjunctam
repraesentationem variorum locorum et temporum, accedis ad
vituperationem ipsarum propter deformitatem valde indecorae mix-
tionis. vituperationis argumentum est ab effecto comoediae ac
tragediae. Concluditur sillog: expli: pri: spe:
Comoedia[26] parit mirificam delectationem, Tragedia excellentem
admirationem.
Nostrorum hominum fabulae non pariunt aut mirificam delectationem, aut excellentem admirationem.
Jtaque nostrorum hominum fabulae neque comoediae sunt neque Tragediae.
Prop: ib: wher the whole.
Assump: ib: So as nether the admiration.
Con: ib: But besides thes grosse absurdities.

Assumptio declaratur et e subjectis enthymemate ⟨declaratis⟩ judicatis,
et e fine.
Nostrorum fabulae proponunt nobis Corydonem Alexandro con-
junctum, continentque aut sola scurrilia, aut effigiem extremae
stultitiae ad eum finem, ut risus excitetur.

Non pariunt igitur excellentem delectationem aut admirationem.
Ante: ib. minglinge kinges. Et ib. So falleth it out. |f. 32|

is, with the play's staging being divided into two days ["True
it is, and so was it to be playd in two daies, and so fitted to
the time it set forth" (198)].

You acknowledge an error in Plautus, while you nevertheless suggest an extenuation from the adjunct, that it is but a single
mistake.

Then there is one more possible objection, this one concerning the
difficulty of representing a history that is made up of various places
and times. But this is refuted from differences:

Tragedy is not tied to the laws of history, but to those of poetry.

A variety of places and times should be narrated, not shown on
stage.

One should not begin *ab ovo*, but from the principal part of the
action to be shown. You illustrate this idea with an example.

Having criticized our writers' plays through the adjunct of their
representing various places and times, you then go on to attack these
same plays for the deformity of their being a highly indecorous mix-
ture. The argument of this attack is from the effect of comedy and
tragedy, concluded in a full syllogism of the first figure:

Comedy gives rise to wondrous delight; tragedy, to a well-raised
admiration.

Our writers' plays do not give rise either to wondrous delight or
to a well-raised admiration.

Thus the plays of our writers are neither comedies nor tragedies.

Proposition: "where the whole tract of a Comedy shoulde be full of
delight, as the Tragedy shoulde be still maintained in a well raised
admiration" (199).

Assumption: "So as neither the admiration and commiseration, nor
the right sportfulnes, is by their mungrell Tragy-comedie obtained"
(199).

Conclusion: "But besides these grosse absurdities, how all theyr Playes
be neither right Tragedies, nor right Comedies" (199).

The Assumption is set forth both from subjects, disposed in an enthymeme, and from the final cause:

Our plays give us Corydon and Alexander together, and they con-
tain either scurrility alone, or an image of utter stupidity with
the end of exciting laughter.

They thus give rise neither to well-raised delight nor to admiration.

Antecedent: "mingling Kings and Clownes" (199), and "So falleth it
out that, hauing indeed no right Comedy, in that comicall part of
our Tragedy we haue nothing but scurrility" (199).

Ad tuendam antecedentem duplex Prolepsis est, Altera de Apuleio, altera de antiquis Comicis. Jllam de Apuleio diversorum argumento antevertis. Hanc de antiquis comicis refellis e facto ipsorum, in vitanda Heroicarum rerum cum levissimis conjunctione.

Antecedentis posterior pars de rebus scurrilibus ad risum excitandum arguitur ab efficiente, nempe opinione quadam in comicis nostris nullam esse sine risu delectationem. Opinio ista facit ut scurrilia et ridicula undique converrant et in fabulas consitiant. Ad hanc opinionem convellendam disputatur de origine delectationis et risus.

Primo e diversis ostenditur risum e delectatione non oriri. ib. For though laughter may come. Diversorum antecedens illustratur adjuncto. Potest enim utrique accidere ut ab eadem re nascatur. ib. But well may.

Deinde est duplex comparatio Dissimilium: in altera notantur dissimilia subjecta e quibus delectatio et risus oriuntur: in altera ponuntur dissimilia adjuncta.
    Prioris dissimilitudinis Protasis. ib. For delighte we scarcely.
    Apodosis ib. Laughter almost.
    Posterioris dissimilitudinis Protasis. ib. Delighte hath a joye.
    Apodosis ib. Laughter hath onlie.
    Vtriusque comparationis partes tractantur inductione specialium.
    ib. For example, we are ravished. |f. 32ᵛ|

Demonstrata origine delectationis et risus e comparatione[27] dissimilium, redis ad docendum illud, posse scilicet delectationem conjungi cum risu. Res docetur ab efficiente:
    Herculis pictura movet delectationem et risum.
    Delectatio, igitur, conjungi potest cum risu.

Anteced: ib. So in Hercules painted. Exornationem habet e simili et

To support this Antecedent you answer two possible objections, the first concerning Apuleius, the second concerning ancient comedians. The objection concerning Apuleius you anticipate by an argument of differences; the second, concerning the ancient comedians, you answer from what they did to avoid mixing heroic things with foolish ones.

The second part of the Antecedent, about scurrilous things meant to excite laughter, is argued from the efficient cause, namely, from a certain opinion among our comedians that there is no delight without laughter. This opinion causes scurrility and foolishness to converge from all sides and end up in dramas. To challenge this opinion, you discuss the true source of delight and laughter.

First you show from an argument of differences that laughter does not originate in delight: "for though laughter may come with delight, yet commeth it not of delight" (199). The first clause of this argument from differences is illustrated from the adjunct; it can in fact happen that both are bred from the same thing: "but well may one thing breed both together" (199).

Next there is a double comparison of unlikes: in one are noted the different subjects from which delight and laughter arise; in the other are set out unlike adjuncts.
   Protasis of the first unlikeness: "for delight we scarcely doe but in things that haue a conueniencie to our selues or to the generall nature" (199). Apodosis: "laughter almost euer commeth of things most disproportioned to our selues and nature" (199).
   Protasis of the second unlikeness: "Delight hath a ioy in it, either permanent or present" (199). Apodosis: "Laughter hath onely a scornful tickling" (199).
   The parts of each comparison are dealt with by an induction of specials: "For example, we are rauished with delight to see a faire woman, and yet are far from being moued to laughter" (199).

Having through this comparison of unlikes demonstrated the origin of delight and laughter, you then go on to show that delight can certainly be joined with laughter. The argument is from the efficient cause:
   The picture of Hercules brings delight and laughter.
   Delight, therefore, can be joined with laughter.

Antecedent: "so in *Hercules*, painted with his great beard and furious countenance, in womans attire, spinning at *Omphales* commaundement, it breedeth both delight and laughter" (200). This is embel-

efficientibus. Simile ib. For as in Alexander. Efficientes ib. For the
  rep'sentinge.
Conse: ib. yet denye J not.
Quinetiam risus iste qui velut finis proponitur fabulis nostrorum
  reprehenditur e subjectis ib. And ye greate faulte. Tum vera subjecta notantur quae risui proponuntur. ib. But rather a busie lo-
  vinge Courtier.
Antequam locum hunc concludis, tu et causam proponis tractationis
  longius productae et quid de Anglorum lyricis sentiendum sit ex-
  ponis. Explicatis lyricarum cantionum veris subjectis, earum usum
  apud Anglos reprehendis duplici argumento, nempe e subjecto et
  e subjecti adjuncta tractatione. Subjectum est Amor. Subjecti adjunctum est frigida et confusa tractatio.

Nostrorum hominum inscitia in rebus Poesi subjectis demonstrata
  jam est: reliquum est ut quid in verbis offendatur ostendas.|f. 33|
Poetarum nostrorum peccatum in verbis ostenditur e verborum adjunctis conclusis enthymemate.
    Verborum, quibus Angli ad Poemata ornanda utuntur, est mirifice
      affectata Rethorica. ib. So is that honieflowinge.
    Jtaque verba nostrorum Poetarum jure vituperanda sunt. ib.
      Nowe for ye out side.
Enthymematis antecedens declaratur e specialibus. Specialia adjuncta verborum sunt.
    Dictiones longe petitae et emendicatae.
    Litterae persequendae studium.
    Figurae et Tropi egentissimi ac frigidissimi.

Peccatum istud poetarum exaggeratur primum e simili facto utentium
  soluta oratione, Academicorum scilicet et Theologorum. Deinde ab
  effecto tuo, id est, optatione quadam ut remotis Nizolianis obser-
  vatimicrilis imitatores Ciceronis et Dimosthenis utrumque oratorem

lished from likeness and from efficient causes. The likeness: "for as in *Alexanders* picture well set out wee delight without laughter" (200). The efficient causes: "For the representing of so strange a power in loue procureth delight: and the scornfulnes of the action stirreth laughter" (200).

Consequent: "Yet deny I not but that they may goe well together" (200).

Next, this laughter which is proposed as the purpose of our plays is criticized from subjects: "And the great fault euen in that point of laughter, and forbidden plainely by *Aristotle*, is that they styrre laughter in sinfull things, which are rather execrable then ridiculous: or in miserable" (200). Then are mentioned the true subjects that create laughter: "But rather a busy louing Courtier, a hartles threatening *Thraso*, a selfe-wise-seeming schoolemaster, a awry-transformed Traueller" (200–201).

Before you finish this topic, you both set forth the cause for your extended treatment of it, and you explain what one should think of English lyric poetry. Once you have outlined the proper subjects for lyrics, you then criticize their use among the English in two arguments, namely, from the subject, and then from the adjunct of the way the subject is handled. The subject is love; the subject's adjunct is love's cold and confused handling.

At this point our writers' ignorance has been demonstrated in the things poetry takes for its subject; what remains is for you to show what is done wrong in language.

The error of our poets in language is shown from the adjuncts of diction, argued in an enthymeme:

> The rhetoric of the words the English use to ornament poems is highly affected: "So is that honny-flowing Matron Eloquence apparelled, or rather disguised, in a Curtizan-like painted affection" (201–02).
>
> Thus the diction of our poets is rightly to be faulted: "Now, for the out-side of it, which is words, or (as I may tearme it) *Diction*, it is euen well worse" (201).

The first term of this enthymeme is set out from specials: the specials are adjuncts of words:

> Expressions are long sought for and changed.
> There is a studious following after the letter.
> Figures and tropes are most meager and cold.

You further develop this offense of poets first from a similarity to what those who use prose have done—academics, for example, and theologians—and then from its effect on you, namely, a certain wish

diligenti versione integrum degustent, et quasi devorent. Optationis
tuae argumentum est a fine: ut scilicet e consuetudine tam accuratae
versionis judicium et prudentiam utriusque Oratoris in Rethoricae
elocutionis usu assequi possimus et imitatione exprimere. Finis iste
dissimili effecto nostrorum hominum exornatur:
Ciceronis et Demosthenis verus imitator judicio quodam, parce
scilicet et nisi suo loco, Rethoricis ornamentis utitur.
At nostri homines conferunt in quamlibet tractationem ornamenta
eloquentiae. |f. 33ᵛ|
Antapodosis exornationem habet e duplici similitudine altera ab iis
qui tractant aromata: altera ab Indis: tum etiam ab exemplis
specialibus ornamentorum, qualia sunt ⟨Epizeuxis⟩ ⌐Anadiplosis⌐ et
similitudo. Jlla sic delectat nostros ut etiam ad familiaris epistolae
ornatum trahatur. Haec e singulis historijs sive herbarum sive
belluarum, volucrum, piscium, ad illuminanda quaevis inventa ingenii nostri eruitur.

Abusus ⟨Epizeuxeos⟩ ⌐Anadiploseos⌐ reprehenditur e fine: quod scilicet
servire debeat iracundae et incensae orationi. Jmmo vero Anadiplosis
non solum inflamatis orationibus sed etiam pacatis dictionibus ser-
vit, ut est in illo vergiliano carmine:
Pierides vos haec facietis maxima Gallo,
Gallo cujus amor tantum crescit in horas.

Abusum similitudinum improbas ab effecto, nempe satietate illa quam
parit frequentissimus earum usus. Effectum istud tractatur e fine
et hoc modo concluditur.

Cujus argumenti usu sola rei illustratio quaeritur, illius argumenti
frequentior usus allata jam illustratione parit satietatem.
At similitudinis usu sola rei illustratio quaeritur.
Jtaque similitudinis frequentior usus facta jam illustratione affert
satietatem.
Prop. deest.
Ass. ib. For the force. arguitur e Diversis.

that the imitators of Cicero and Demosthenes, free from Nizolian paper-books, would taste and as it were devour the whole of each author through attentive translation.[54] The argument concerning your wish is from final cause, that through the habit of so attentive a translation we could acquire the judgment and prudence that each of these orators had in using the elocution of rhetoric, and that we could express these qualities through imitation. This purpose is further developed from how the effect of our writers is different:

The true imitator of Cicero and Demosthenes, through a certain judgment, uses rhetorical ornaments sparingly, and only in their proper place;

But our writers put ornaments of eloquence in any sort of writing.

The second term of this enthymeme is developed in a double simile, whose first part concerns those who use spices, and whose second part concerns Indians. You then give special examples of ornament, such as anadiplosis [i.e., repetition] and simile. The first of these so delights our writers that it is even used to ornament a familiar epistle; the second is rifled up out of certain discourses, whether of herbs, or beasts, or birds, or fish, to illustrate any sort of invention of our wit.

The abuse of anadiplosis is criticized from final cause, that it ought to be used, that is, for an enraged and incensed oration. (On the contrary, anadiplosis is in fact good not just for inflamed orations, but also for peaceful expressions, as in that Virgilian song:

O Muses, make the most to Gallus of these lines,

Gallus, for whom my love grows by the hour. [Eclogue X. 11. 72–73])[55]

You criticize the abuse of simile from effect, namely from that satiety that too-frequent use of them brings about. This effect is dealt with from its final cause, and is set out like this:

Where the only thing aimed for in using an argument is the explanation of something, to use it further once an explanation has been made creates satiety.

But in using a simile, the only thing that is aimed for is the explanation of something.

Thus, further use of simile once an explanation has been made creates satiety.

Proposition: omitted.

Assumption: "for the force of a similitude not being to prooue anything to a contrary Disputer but onely to explane to a willing hearer" (203). It is argued from differences.

Con. ib. When that is done. Ad cujus exornationem subjicitur com-
paratio e majoribus. |f. 34|

Similitudo (clarissime Sidneie) non est Rethoricae elocutionis ornamentum, sed Logicae inventionis argumentum: quia inest in similitudine
vis quaedam ad rem arguendam et declarandam.
Porro abusum hunc Rethoricorum ornamentorum, quem Poetae induxerunt nostri, comparatione dissimilium amplificas. ib. For my
part. Deinde Collatione Minorum. ib. vndoubtedly at least. Collationem e minoribus illustras exposita causa cur id et ab ⟨aliquo⟩
ᴿaulicoᴸ et ab Academico praestetur. Quod cum feceris, Prolepsin
adversus digressionem istam a Poesi ad Oratoriam refellis e fine;
ut nempe quid a te dicatur digressionis istius beneficio intelligatur,
id est, ut communis contagionis unam alteramve labem ostendas.
Finis iste arguitur ab efficiente, videlicet utriusque artis cognatione.
Tum e Diversis ib. wᶜʰ is not to take uppon me.

Hic ad laudationem digrederis Linguae Anglicanae.
Primo linguam Anglicam vindicas ab objectis contumeliis. Objicitur
ad laudem Linguae Anglicanae minuendam Linguae Anglicanae
Materia ex qua concrevit: id est, perigrinorum idiomatum varietas.
Respondetur huic objectioni ab Adjuncta praestantia assumptae ex
alijs idiomatis materiae:
    Assumpta ad nostram Linguam ex alijs idiomatis materia est, quae
    erat in alijs idiomatis longe optima. ib. Takinge the best.
Jtaque Lingua nostra concreta ex hujusmodi materia excellit. ib.
    And why not. |f. 34ᵛ|
Objicitur praeterea nulla esse posse Grammatica praecepta Anglici
idiomatis. Respondetur e contradictionis argumento esse posse. con-
tradictionem tuam exornas e Diversis:

Conclusion: "when that is done, the rest is a most tedious pratling" (203). You add a comparison from the greater to ornament this.

A simile (most eminent Sidney) is not an ornament of rhetorical eloquence, but an argument of logical invention, since there is in simile a certain force for arguing and explaining something.[56]
Then, from a comparison of unlikes, you amplify this abuse of rhetorical ornaments that our poets have brought about: "For my part, I doe not doubt, when *Antonius* and *Crassus*, the great forefathers of *Cicero* in eloquence, the one (as *Cicero* testifieth of them) pretended not to know Arte, the other not to set by it . . . — I doe not doubt (I say) but that they vsed these tracks very sparingly" (203). Then from a comparison from the lesser: "Vndoubtedly (at least to my opinion vndoubtedly) I haue found in diuers smally learned Courtiers a more sounde stile then in some professors of learning" (203). You illustrate this comparison from the lesser by explaining why the abuse shows so clearly both at court and at school. Then, when you have done this, you answer from final cause a possible objection against this digression of yours from poetry to oratory. You digress, that is, in order that your digression should be understood as something helpful; in particular, so that you can show one or another blot of common contagion. This end is argued from the efficient cause (which is to say, your own connection to each art), and then from an argument of differences: "which is not to take vpon me to teach Poets howe they should doe, but onely, finding my selfe sick among the rest, to shewe some one or two spots of the common infection" (203-4).

Here you digress in praise of the English language.
First you clear English from the slanders laid against it. To diminish the praise of English, the matter is criticized from which English took shape, i.e., a variety of foriegn languages. You respond to this objection from the adjunct of the excellence of what has been borrowed from other languages:
> The matter taken from foreign languages for our language was by far the best of those other languages: "taking the best of both the other" (204).
> Thus our language, made up of this kind of matter, excels: "And why not so much the better, taking the best of both the other?" (204).
It is also objected that there can be no grammar of English. You answer with a contradiction that there can be. You embellish your contradiction from an argument of differences:

Etiamsi tradi potest Grammatica Anglici idiomatis, tamen tradi
eam non est necesse.
Diversorum posteriorem partem probas ab Adjuncto:
Jnest in Anglicano idiomate naturalis facilitas. ib. Beinge so
easie.
Jtaque[28] non eget praeceptis grammaticis. ib. But it needes
it not.

Antecedentis confirmatio est ab efficiente facilitatis nempe defectu
casuum, generum, modorum et temporum. Vbi est exornatio ab
Adjuncto harum proprietatum quod nimirum earum unaquaeque
sit pars illius poenae quam ⌐turri⌐ Babilonicae inflixit Deus.

Carere voces Anglicanas casuum et modorum differentiis, in eo tibi
assentior. De generum vero et temporum defectu assentiri non
possum, ut cons[tat his] exemplis: He, she; Kinge, Queene: Lord[,]
Ladye: Maister, Mistres: Husband, Wife: Edward, Elizabeth[:]
Gander, Goose: Drake, Ducke. Quod ad tempora attinet: habent
etiam verba nostra sua tempora, praesertim praesens et praeteritum.
ut Teache, Toughte: Prove, Proved: Refute[,] Refuted[:] Desire[,]
Desired: Heare, He⌐a⌐rde: Have, Had: am, was: quod idem in aliis
verbis licet deprehendere. |f. 35|
Sed differentiarum istarum unamquamque vis esse partem divinae
poenae. At cur has potius quam illas numeri et personae? Deinde
quaero quî id possit esse vindictae divinae pars quod tempore vin-
dictam divinam antecessit? Cadunt enim differentiae istae in
Linguam Haebraeam. At Lingua Haebraea vincit antiquitate turrim Babilonicam. Ego certe non istas proprietates, quibus suam
linguam a principio ornavit Deus etiam tum cum Adamum allo-
queretur, sed potius nominum notationem partim sublatam, partim obscuratam et confusam statuo esse partem poenae illius, qua
turrim Babilonicam affecit Deus.

Duplici Prolepsi refutata laudas Anglicum sermonem.
Primum a comparatione Parium ib. But for the utteringe.
Deinde ab Adjuncto quarundum vocum, nempe compositione.
ib. and is particularlye. Adjunctum istud comparatione ma-

Even though an English grammar could be written, still it is not
necessary that one be written.

You argue the second part of this argument of differences from
the adjunct:

> There is in English a natural easiness: "beeing so easie of it
> selfe, and so voyd of those cumbersome differences of Cases,
> Genders, Moodes, and Tenses, which I thinke was a peece
> of the Tower of *Babilons* curse, that a man should be put
> to schoole to learne his mother-tongue" (204).

Therefore it needs no grammar: "but it needes it not" (204).

The confirmation of the first term of this argument is from the efficient cause of this uneasiness, namely, the lack in English of cases,
genders, moods, and tenses. The development here is from the adjunct of these properties, specifically, that each of them is part of
the punishment God inflicted at the Tower of Babel.

I agree with you that English expressions lack differences of cases and
moods, but surely I cannot agree about a lack of genders or tenses,
as in these examples: He, She; King, Queene; Lord, Lady; Maister,
Mistress; Husband, Wife; Edward, Elizabeth; Gander, Goose;
Drake, Ducke. With respect to tenses, our verbs have as their tenses
especially present and preterite, as in: Teach, Toughte; Prove,
Proved; Refute, Refuted; Desire, Desired; Heare, Hearde; Have,
Had; Am, Was. The same may be seen in other verbs.

But you want all of these differences of yours to be part of the divine
punishment. But why these differences instead of those of number
and person? Moreover, I ask how something that precedes that
divine punishment would yet be a part of that same divine punishment? For these differences occur in Hebrew, and Hebrew antedates
the Tower of Babel. I believe that it is surely not these properties
(with which God ornamented his language from the very beginning, when Adam spoke), but rather that etymology of names, partly hidden, partly obscure and confused, that is a part of that punishment with which God struck the Tower of Babel.

With the two-fold objection refuted, you praise English speech:

> First from a comparison of equals: "But for the vttering sweetly
> and properly the conceits of the minde, which is the end of
> speech, that hath it equally with any other tongue in the world"
> (204).

> Then you praise from the adjunct of certain sounds, particularly
> as they can be linked together: "and is particulerly happy in com-
> positions of two or three words together" (204). This adjunct

jorum et minorum commendatur. ib. neare the Greeke.
Tum ab adjuncta facultate, qua aptus est ad omne genus metri.
ib. Truelie the Englishe before. Hic tu exornationem subjecisti
e distributione metricae disciplinae ⌐in⌐ duas partes, e definitione utriusque partis, denique e comparatione utriusque. ib.
Nowe of versafienge. Porro adjunctae hujus facultatis alia exornatio est e comparationibus minorum. Facis enim caeterarum
|f. 35ᵛ| gentium vulgaria idiomata vinci ab Anglicano, facultate
illa quae metricae disciplinae utriusque speciebus inservit. ib.
For for the ancient. et ib. Nowe for the Rime.

Pervenimus ad totius Epilogum disputationis tuae: quem tu pro ingenio singulari ornas more Rethorum. Habet enim nitorem variae
Elocutionis in Troporum luminibus et concinnitate Figurarum. Sed
Epilogi Logica non minus elegans est. Hortaris omnes qui disputationem istam De Poesi tuam in manus sumpserunt, ut Poesin excellens quoddam et divinum munus esse putent. Hortationis
argumentum est
    Ab effecto. ib. So that since.
    ab Adjuncto. ib. And voide of noe.
    ab adjuncta innocentia. ib. Since the blames laide.
    ab efficiente contemptus illius quo Angli erga Poetas tenentur.
    ib. since the cause why it is.
    ab Adjuncto Anglici idiomatis, quod comparatione tractatur. ib.
    Since lastely our Tounge. |f. 36|

Quintuplex istud argumentum enthymemate concluditur:

    Poesis parit delectationem illam quae est author virtutis.
    Instructa est omnibus iis muneribus, quae cadunt in naturam artis.

is praised in a comparison of the greater and the lesser: "neere the Greeke, far beyond the Latine" (204).

Then English is praised from the adjunct of the faculty that makes it fit for every kind of meter: "Truely the English, before any other vulgar language I know, is fit for both sorts" (204–5). Here you have added ornamentation from a distribution of metrics into two parts, then from a definition of each part, and then from a comparison of each: "Now, of versifying there are two sorts, the one Auncient, the other Moderne" (204). Finally, through comparisons from the lesser, you embellish further the adjunct of this faculty, for you suggest that English surpasses the common languages of all other peoples through having that faculty that serves versifying of both kinds: "for, for the Ancient, the Italian is so full of Vowels that it must euer be cumbred with *Elisions*; the Dutch so, of the other side, with Consonants, that they cannot yeeld the sweet slyding fit for a Verse" (205); and "Nowe, for the ryme, though wee doe not obserue quantity, yet wee obserue the accent very precisely: which other languages eyther cannot doe or will not doe so absolutely" (205).

We have finally arrived at the epilogue of your whole disputation, which you ornament with singular genius, just like a rhetorician. Truly it has a brilliance of varied elocution in ornaments of tropes and the polish of figures. But the logic of the epilogue is no less elegant. You urge all who have taken this, your disputation *On Poetry*, in hand, to believe that poetry is a certain excellent and divine gift. The argument of this exhortation is:

from effect: "So that sith the euer-praise-worthy Poesie is full of vertue-breeding delightfulnes" (205);

from adjunct: "and voyde of no gyfte that ought to be in the noble name of learning" (205);

from the adjunct of innocence: "sith the blames laid against it are either false or feeble" (205);

from the efficient cause of that contempt which the English hold for poets: "sith the cause why it is not esteemed in Englande is the fault of Poet-apes, not Poets" (205);

from the adjunct of the English tongue, dealt with in a comparison: "sith, lastly, our tongue is most fit to honor Poesie" (205).

This five-part argument is concluded in an enthymeme:

Poetry breeds the delight that is the source of virtue.
Poetry has been provided with all those gifts that fall within the nature of art.

Contumelia objecta poetis vel falsa est vel imbecilitate sua concidit.
Non Poetae sed stulti imitatores Poetarum Poesin in contemptum
   vocaverunt.
Lingua nostra est et aptissima ad Poesin ornandam et dignissima
   quae ornetur ab eadem.

Ergo Poesin excellens quoddam et divinum munus esse putate.
Anteced. ib. so that since. estque superioribus repetita.
conse: ib. J conjure y^u all.
conclusio ista habet amplificationem e varijs diversis. Diversorum pars
   prior. ib. No more to scorne.
   posterior. ib. But to beleve wth Aristotle, Bembus, Scaliger,[29]
   Clawçer, Landin.
Hortationis aliud argumentum est ab adjunctis commodis, quae
   Poeseos amorem seq^{r}u^{1}ntura sunt. ib. Thus doing y^{er} name shall
   florishe. |f. 36^v|
Hortationis postremum argumentum est ab Adjuncta imprecatione.
   ib. But if fie on suche a but. Jmprecatio tractatur argumento
   diversorum.

Hactenus subduxi analysin inventionis tuae (praestantissime Sidneie)
   judicii etiam in enuntiato & syllogismo. Restat analysis Methodi.
   Ut es in argumentis excogitandis peracutus, in judicio enuntiati &
   syllogismi persubtilis: sic es in methodica rerum collocatione non
   parum accuratus: utcunque in nonnullis methodi χρύψιν adhibueris.
   Primo totius tractationis summum ac velut definitionem proponis,
   dum ais te aggredi defensionem poeseos. Deinde ipsam tractationem
   instituis. Jn quo es legi methodi obsecutus. Nam res ad tractandam
   subjecta est prior & generalior ipsa tractatione. si illa extiterit, non
   sequitur hanc esse. at si haec fuerit, illam praecessisse sequitur.

The blame laid on poets is either false, or it collapses of its own
  weakness.
Not poets, but dull imitators of poets, have brought poetry to
  disgrace.
Our tongue is both most fit to honor poetry, and most worthy
  of being honored by poetry.

Believe, therefore, that poetry is a certain excellent and divine gift.

Antecedent: "So that sith" and what has been given above.

Consequent: "I coniure you all that haue had the euill lucke to reade
  this incke-wasting toy of mine, euen in the name of the nyne Muses,
  no more to scorne the sacred misteries of Poesie" (205–6).

This conclusion is amplified from various differences. The partition
  of these differences:

   prior: "no more to scorne the sacred misteries of Poesie, no more
     to laugh at the name of Poets, as though they were next in-
     heritours to Fooles, no more to iest at the reuerent title of a
     Rymer" (206).

   posterior: "but to beleeue, with *Aristotle*, that they were the aun-
     cient Treasurers of the Graecians Diuinity" (206).

Another argument of your exhortation is from the adjuncts of the ad-
  vantages that will follow the love of poetry: "Thus doing, your name
  shal florish in the Printers shoppes" (206).

The last argument of the exhortation is from the adjunct of imprecation: "But if (fie of such a but) you be borne so neere the dull making *Cataphract* of *Nilus* that you cannot heare the Plannet-like Musick
  of Poetrie" (206). The imprecation is dealt with in an argument of
  differences.

To this point (most worthy Sidney) I have provided an analysis of your
invention, and also of your judgment in axiom and in syllogism.
The analysis of method remains to be done.[57] Just as you are most
acute in thinking through arguments, and most precise in judging
axiom and syllogism, so you are no less careful in methodical
organization, though you have used some crypsis of method. At the
beginning you set the chief goal and as it were the definition of your
whole treatise when you say you undertake the defense of poetry.
Next you set up the treatise itself. In this you have followed the law
of method. For the subject to be treated is prior to and more general
than the treatise itself. If the first of these exists, then it does not
necessarily follow that the second does. But if this second exists, it
follows that the first has preceded.[58]

Tractatio[30] tua ad laudem Poeseos sita est partim in confirmatione veritatis: partim in refutatione calumniae. Primo veritatem confirmas: tum calumniam refellis. Quid potest esse in methodica rerum dispositione accuratius? Rei veritas est prior iis omnibus quae adversus veritatem objiciuntur. si enim quid calumniae commentive contra rei veritatem objicitur, necesse est rei veritatem existere. at si rei veritas sit, non sequitur calumniam aliquam esse. Quid quod rei veritas sit subjectum? allata contra rei veritatem objectio adjunctum? at subjectum adjuncto prius est & generalius. |f. 37|
Jn persequenda confirmatione veritatis primo laudas Poesin, a triplici adjuncto, nimirum antiquitate, communitate, nominibus. Deinde eandem definis. Hîc igitur a lege methodi descivisti & κρύψιν adhibuisti. Poeseos definitio est praeponenda explicationi adjunctorum. Subjectum enim est adjunctis generalius ac prius. Si poesis sit, non sequitur illa adjuncta esse, at si illa adjuncta fuerint, sequetur poesin esse. Quinetiam adjunctorum intelligentia erit difficilima, nisi prius constiterit & intelligatur quid sit illud, cujus adjuncta sunt.
A poeseos definitione ad ejusdem distributionem accedis. methodi lex id quidem postulat, nisi quid occurrat singularum partium commune. distributionis partes facis tres, quarum alia est posita in exprimendis Dei excellentiis, alia in explicatione philosophiae, alia in rerum fictione. Quod tractationem rerum verè existentium praeponas rerum fictioni, facis accommodatè ad praeceptum methodi. Quod vero de poesi rerum divinarum ante disseras quam de poesi philosophiae humanae, in eo aberratum est a methodo. Nam philosophiae humanae cognitio multum lucis affert ad intelligentiam divinae naturae. poesis igitur humanae philosophiae, quia notior est & illustrior, ideo praeponenda est poesi Divinae naturae: alioqui methodus ab ignotioribus ad notiora progrederetur.

Tertiam poeseos partem situm in rebus fingendis primo describis: deinde in membra dividis. tum de adjuncto vestimento & effectis disputas. Atqui vero |f. 37ᵛ| quod ad singula distributionis mem-

Your treatise in praise of poetry consists partly in a confirmation of its true nature, partly in a refutation of calumny. First you confirm its true nature; then you refute calumny. What can be more correct in disposing something by method? The true nature of something is prior to everything that can be objected to its true nature. For if a calumny or a lie is raised against the true nature of something, then it is necessary that the true nature of the thing exist. But if the true nature of a thing should exist, it does not follow that some sort of calumny exists. What other reason could there be that the true nature of something should be a subject, or that an objection raised against that true nature should be an adjunct? And a subject is prior to and more general than an adjunct.

In carrying out the confirmation of poetry's true nature, you first praise poetry from three adjuncts, specifically, from antiquity, community, and names. Then you define it. Here, then, you have departed from the law of method and you have used crypsis. The definition of poetry ought to be put before the explanation of its adjuncts, because a subject is more general than its adjuncts, and prior to them. Given that poetry exists, it does not follow that these adjuncts exist; but if these adjuncts should exist, it will follow that poetry exists. And thus the understanding of adjuncts will be most difficult, unless it should first be well-established and understood what that thing could be to which the adjuncts belong.

From the definition of poetry you proceed to the distribution of it. The law of method in fact requires that step, unless something should come up that is common to all the individual parts. You give three parts in the distribution, one of which is defined by its expressing the excellences of God, another by its explaining philosophy, the last by its feigning things. When you place the treatment of things which actually exist before the treatment of fictional things, you proceed in accord with the precept of method. But certainly when you treat divine poetry before the poetry of human philosophy, there you make an error in method. For the knowledge of human philosophy brings much light to the understanding of divinity. Thus the poetry of human philosophy, since it is more known and more clear, is on that account to be put before the poetry of divinity. Otherwise, method would proceed from the lesser known to the more known.

You first describe the third part of poetry as being in the feigning of things, and then you divide it into its members. Then you discuss the adjunct both of a poem's "dress" and its effects. But surely, whatever pertains generally to individual members of a distribution

bra generatim attinet, id ex lege methodi ante explicandum est, quam ipsa membra singillatim explicantur. Equidem & apparatus ille quo poesis vestitur & effecta illa quae a poesi proficiscuntur, sunt ad singula distributionis membra fusa communiter. Ac proinde distributioni praeponi debuerunt.

Confirmata veritate aggrederis refutationem calumniae. in qua illae calumniae, quae sunt de effecto poeseos, prius refellendae sunt quam illae quae sunt de poeseos adjunctis.

Quod si quis velit totius tractationis methodum accuratius informare, poterit hujusmodi adumbrationem afferre.

    Aggredior defensionem poeseos.

        Poesis est ars fictionis ad docendum & delectandum. Eam ego statuo caeteris disciplinis antiquiorem esse. Video coli illam non modo a politioribus populis sed etiam a barbaris & agrestibus nationibus. Qui ad illius studium se totos retulerunt, ii vatis & poetae nomen consecuti sunt.

        Poesis[31] alia sita est in tractatione rerum verè existentium, alia in rerum fictione. Quae res verè existentes tractat, illa in explicatione philosophiae aut divinae naturae versatur.

        Poesis quae in rebus fingendis posita est, illi priori non minus dissimilis ᶜest⁷ quam mediocris pictor |f. 38| excellenti & qui hanc colunt ii merito poetae appellantur.

Quod si quis eam cum caeteris artibus conferat, vincit illa quidem, si theologiam exceperis, reliquas omnes facultate quadam homines ad summum bonum perducendi. Nam virtutem hominibus tradit & praecepto & exemplo: eamque sic eleganter velut ad oculum depingit, ut illius in hominum mentibus mirabilem amorem excitet. Atque ut dignitate materiae, sic etiam vestimenti genere reliquis disciplinis antecellit. ideoque oratione numeris astricta vestiri vult.

Poesis duplex est. alia versatur in rebus levioribus, alia in gravioribus. Quae tractat res leviores, illa utitur perpetua oratione vel mutuo colloquio. Quae perpetua oratione utitur, occupata est in reprehensione vel deploratione. quae occupata est in reprehensione, ea reprehendit improbitatem acerbè, ut Iambica: aut stultitiam facetè, ut Satyra. quae occupata est in deploratione, dicitur Elegia.

Jam vero quae utitur mutuo colloquio in rebus levioribus est Bucolica

is by the law of method to be explained before those members are themselves explained separately. Certainly, both that garment in which poetry is dressed, and those effects which proceed from poetry, extend to all of the individual members of the distribution, and thus they ought to have been put before the distribution.[59]

With the true nature of poetry confirmed, you go on to the refutation of calumny, where those calumnies that concern the effect of poetry are to be answered before those that concern the adjuncts of poetry.

But if anyone should want to make the method of the whole treatise more accurate, he could suggest something like this:[60]

I undertake the defense of poetry.

Poetry is an art of fiction-making, for teaching and delighting. I claim it to be older than other arts. I see that it is cultivated not just by the more civilized peoples, but also by barbarous and wild nations. Those who have given themselves wholly to the study of poetry have attained the name of *vates* and "poet."

Some poetry consists in dealing with truly existing things; some consists in feigning things. That which deals with truly existing things is engaged in explaining either philosophy or divinity.

Poetry that consists in feigning things is to the first kind no less unlike than is the average painter to the excellent one, and those who cultivate this poetry are by merit called "poets."[61]

But if someone were to compare this art to other arts, poetry certainly surpasses them all, if you except theology, by means of a certain capacity it has to lead men to the highest good. For it teaches virtue to men both by precept and example, and it depicts virtue so elegantly to the eye that it excites in men's minds a marvellous love of that virtue. And as in the value of its subject, so also with respect to the way it is dressed, it excels the other disciplines, and for that reason, it wants to be dressed in meter. Poetry has two parts: one deals with lighter matters, the other with more serious matters. The part that treats lighter matters uses either continuous speech or dialogue. The one that uses continuous speech is concerned with either reprehending or lamenting. The part that is concerned with reprehending criticizes dishonesty harshly, as Iambic verse; when it deals humorously with folly, it is as a Satire. The part concerned with lamenting is called Elegy. Then, surely, the poetry that uses dialogue for lighter matters is either Pastoral or Comedy. Poetry

vel Comoedia. Poesis sita in rebus gravioribus continet imitationem excellentis vitii aut historiam insignis virtutis. illa est tragaedia: haec heroica aut lyrica. Quod si poesis reprehendenda est, harum aliquam vituperandam esse constat. at si unamquamque singillatim excusseris intelliges unamquamque in summa laude ponendam esse. Verum demonstratio |f. 38ᵛ| ista levior esse videbitur, nisi & refellantur ea quae contra afferri possunt. Calumniae contra poesin allatae sunt de effectis poeseos aut adjunctis. sed utriusque generis calumnia levissima est. Quamobrem cum & laudes illae, quas poesi attribuerim, justissimae sint, & calumniae, quae in illam a sycophantis conferuntur, levissimae: hortor eos omnes, qui istam de poesi tractationem in manus sumpturi sunt, ut poesin divinum quoddam & excellens munus esse arbitrentur.

Habes jam (illustrissime Philippe) analysin totius tractationis tuae, siue inventionis argumenta spectes, siue judicii vim consideres. Habes etiam adumbrationem quandam methodi, ad cujus rationem tractatio conformanda est. Quod si in subducenda analysi aliquid minus accuratum praestiterim, erit dignitatis tuae & ignoscere id in quo offenditur & sperare deinceps meliora.

given to graver matters deals either with the imitation of an outstanding failing, or with a story of noble virtue. The first is Tragedy,
the second is either Epic or Lyric.

Then if poetry is to be criticized, it is clear that at least one of
these parts is to be attacked. But if you should excuse each of these
parts individually, then you will see that every one is to be given
the highest praise. Of course this demonstration will seem rather
weak unless those things that can be argued against poetry are also
refuted. Calumnies against poetry are related either to the effects
of poetry, or to its adjuncts. But a calumny of either sort is most
insubstantial. Thus, both because these praises I have given poetry
are most just, and because the calumnies brought against it by
slanderers are most insubstantial, I urge all those who will take this
treatise on poetry in hand to judge that poetry is a certain divine
and excellent gift.

You now have (most excellent Philip) an analysis of your whole treatise,
whether you look at arguments of invention, or whether you consider strength of judgment. You also have a certain outline of
method, to whose order the treatise should be organized.[62] But if
in the analysis raised here I should have suggested anything that
is less than accurate, it will be characteristic of your nobleness both
to pardon whatever gives offense, and to hope for better in the future.

Textual Notes

1. *Stagyra*] *Stagyras* MS.
2. MS begins *Laudandus* as a sub-subparagraph.
3. Temple's citation differs from O, P, N and Pe. Cf. citation given in the translation.
4. *genere*] *ge-/re* MS (hyphenated across line end).
5. *fictitiam?*] *fictitiam.* MS.
6. *diversis*] *diveris* MS.
7. *essentialis*] *essentia* MS (There is below this insertion a cancelled word, which is blotted to illegibility).
8. Citation differs from O, P, N, Pe. Cf. translation.
9. MS fails to indent *Deinde*.
10. MS omits the Conclusion which should follow this Proposition and Assumption.
11. The indentations shown here reflect the MS. Temple normally shows no indentation in quoting to illustrate an outlined syllogism. He allows himself the same inconsistencies on [f. 23] and [f. 26].
12. Citation differs from O, P, N, Pe. Cf. translation.
13. The sentence beginning *Porro poetam* is squeezed into the extra interlinear space between this paragraph and the following line. It was clearly added after the copyist had proceeded beyond this point in the text.
14. Citation differs from O, P, N, Pe. Cf. translation.
15. Citation differs from O, P, N, Pe. Cf. translation.
16. In transliterating "praxis" Temple differs from the extant MSS N and Pe, and from P. Because everywhere else he retains Greek letters, it is hard to know whether the MS he was working from showed transliterations.
17. Citation differs from O, P, N, Pe. Cf. translation.
18. Citation differs from O, P, N, but agrees with Pe. Cf. translation.
19. MS fails to establish new line with *Memoria*.
20. MS shows *subjectum* as a sub-subparagraph, and fails to indent the following enthymeme.
21. MS begins *sequitur* as a subparagraph, and fails to set the line off from what precedes it with an extra interlinear space.
22. MS fails to establish new line with *ideoque*.
23. *causis,*] *causis.* MS.
24. Citation differs from O, P, N, Pe. Cf. translation.
25. Hand B begins here. The change in format convention reflects the MS.
26. *Comoedia*] *Comadia* MS (Hand B's digraph is often very faint, but his

spelling seems inconsistent between *comoedia, comaedia, comadia*. All forms in [ff. 31v–36] have been regularized to *comoedia*).

27. *comparatione*] *compara-/ratione* MS (hyphenated across line end).

28. MS begins *Jtaque* as a subparagraph, instead of as the more consistent sub-subparagraph.

29. Scaliger] Caliger MS.

30. MS begins *Tractatio* as a subparagraph.

31. Temple's format grows irregular at this point, as if he is not completely sure that hierarchical indentations are necessary to this section. The MS begins *Poesis alia* as a sub-sub-subparagraph (the deepest subordination of the entire MS), suggesting the logical subordination of this section to the preceding definition of poetry, but then Temple begins his next paragraph, *Poesis quae*, as only a subparagraph. Then at [f. 38] he virtually abandons the outline format entirely, maintaining only the first level indentation of the hang-indent main paragraph style. I have regularized the paragraphing, and I have maintained the outline format through the end of the carry-over sentence from [f. 37v], but beginning with *Quod si* I follow the MS.

Notes to the Translation

1. I.e., see how Virgil conquered Aristotle and Plato. Virgil was born in Mantua, Aristotle was born in Stagyra, and Plato's Academy was held in a plane tree grove. Temple's point is to praise Sidney for having (like Virgil) redeemed poetry from attacks upon it by philosophy.

2. I.e., Apollo's laurel bough. Apollo was Latona's son.

3. *On Poetry.* In referring to Sidney's work Temple capitalizes *de Poesi* as a title five times. He does so here in the title, again in the first line, on [f. 12] (*de Poesi*) and [ff. 7v and 35v] (*De Poesi*). Sidney seems never to have given his work a title; *An Apologie for Poesie* and *The Defense of Poetry* are titles contributed after Sidney's death by the work's early editors. Given the silence on the matter by all other printings and manuscripts, it is unlikely that Temple's title is an earlier title of Sidney's own invention. More probably it is Temple's imposition for ease of reference.

4. In the Ramist system, the truth of an "axiom," or statement, can be judged either by axiomatical judgment or by syllogistic judgment. In axiomatical judgment, one inspects the statement, and if it is so clear that anyone can see its obvious truth, then there will be no need to employ syllogism. Thus syllogistic judgment functions like a court of appeal for more difficult cases. Temple's praise here is to remark that Sidney's opening arguments are — as Temple thinks opening remarks should be — so clear that they are self-evident, and therefore in no need of the kind of syllogistic demonstration that will be used later. See the Introduction, part I for a more complete description of the role of judgment.

5. The Consequent which should follow this Antecedent has already been cited in the preceding Apodosis: "So haue I need to bring some more auaileable proofes" (151).

6. The citation Temple gives here as the Proposition contains as well the Conclusion to this syllogism: "they goe very neer to vngratefulnes" (151).

7. The columns Temple refers to are described by Flavius Josephus in *The Antiquities of the Jews*, Chapter 2. Seth's children "were the inventors of that peculiar sort of wisdom which is concerned with the heavenly bodies and their order. And, that their inventions might not be lost before they were sufficiently known, upon Adam's prediction that the world was to be destroyed at one time by the force of *fire*, and at another time by the violence and quantity of *water*, they made two pillars; the one of brick, the other of stone; they inscribed their discoveries on them both ...." (From *The Works of Flavius Josephus*, trans. William Whiston [Philadelphia, 1832], 1:15.) Temple thinks it unlikely that poets lived before the flood, and thus, since these pre-flood columns could

not have been inscribed unless something was already known, Temple doubts that poetry could be older than all other disciplines.

8. *Species*. Two terms Temple uses somewhat inconsistently are "species" and "specials," where a "special" would be a unique member of a "species." Thus Epic would be a "species" of poetry, but Homer's poetry would be a "special" case of the species "Epic." Temple never uses "special" where "species" would be more appropriate, but at several points he uses "species" where "special" would be more precise.

9. The division Temple makes here is between a cause which simply brings one to learning, "admiration," in this case, and a cause which actually creates learning in the first place. Though the argument here is historical, the issue of what "causes" learning is important to both Sidney and Temple, and is raised again when Temple denies that poetry teaches better than philosophy does because it moves us better. See p. 115 below.

10. Temple has cited the Consequent to follow this Antecedent earlier on p. 67: "[they] went before them as causes to drawe with their charming sweetnes the vntamed wits to an admiration of knowledge."

11. Sidney does not actually pose the question Temple gives as the Consequent ("So who will doubt the praise of poetry?"). Temple takes it to be implicit.

12. Temple's point is that many things which no one would praise are widely diffused, as for example perverse opinions of God. Thus it is wrong to conclude, as Sidney does, that poetry is to be praised simply for its being cultivated widely.

13. By "efficient causes of the name" Temple means that men were caused to apply the name *vates* by virtue of the artist's capacity to foretell events, and that they were caused to apply the name "poet" by virtue of the artist's capacity to "make" (*poiein* in Greek) things.

14. I.e., "what the Roman Emperors did" was to give poets the name *Vates*, or "seer," in recognition of their divine inspiration. Thus because David was also divinely inspired, the fact that he wrote in verse supports the appropriateness of the action Roman Emperors took in giving poets the name *Vates*.

15. The etymology is from effect because the fact that poets "made" things caused the Greeks to name them "poets," or "makers," and therefore the name "poet" is the effect of having seen artists as "makers."

16. Ramist rhetorics have two parts, Elocution and Delivery; tropes and figures are the two branches of Elocution. Rhetoric's defining goal in this system is only to make speech or writing attractive and forceful. Doing this may in fact turn out to be persuasive, but that, as Temple says a few lines later, will be only a fortuitous or contingent result, and thus persuasion cannot be the primary end of the art, since persuasion will not always result from rhetoric, even when it is used properly and well.

17. Logic's true end is to discourse well (*bene disserere*), and doing that requires solely the proper invention and the proper judging of arguments. Though the clarity with which logic presents ideas may be persuasive, it is not necessarily so, and thus when persuasion does result from logic, it does so only fortuitously. Temple's point is that Sidney is wrong to say that the rhetorician and the logician consider "what in Nature will soonest ... perswade." In what now follows, Temple makes a similar objection to Sidney's definition of metaphysics, arguing

that the characteristics Sidney identifies with metaphysics belong instead to natural philosophy.

18. "Matter" and "form" as the two determinates of all physical objects have both Aristotle's and Plato's authority. Just as a craftsman creates an object by imposing a form on his otherwise unformed clay, so nature creates its objects by imposing a form on a basic, inchoate *prima materia*. Neither "form" nor "matter" can exist in nature without the other; neither can be seen except as they are combined in a particular physical entity. Thus even if nature's objects are themselves concrete, in trying to establish what any particular object's true "form" or "matter" is, the natural philosopher's task is very much an abstract art.

19. Temple's language here echoes Ramus' description of the *Metaphysics* as "scattered heaps of inane uncertainties" (*inanium dubitationum cumuli substrati*). Ramus thought Aristotle's Metaphysics to be a confused collection of many disparate subjects. See *Aristotelicae Animadversiones* (Paris, 1543), pp. 63 a/b, 64a.

20. Literally: to separate astronomy and music from natural philosophy "is not consistent with the Law of Justice." By this Temple means that the two arts of astronomy and music are both members of the set of arts that make up natural philosophy, and that to list them (as Sidney does) along with natural philosophy as if all three were equal and independent arts fails to respect the integrity of natural philosophy's subject matter. See Laws of Truth, Justice, and Wisdom in the Glossary.

21. Crypsis of method. Method in Ramist logic was of two classes, "natural," and "cryptic" (or "prudential"). Natural Method, described above in the Introduction, part 1, was supposed to be the clearest way to organize axioms. But in a number of circumstances one could abandon its hierarchical structure. This would be done by inverting orders, even to the point of hiding one's true intent. Such inversions, or "crypses," could be designed to give pleasure, as when the epic poet begins *in medias res*, or they could be used to deceive or entrap an antagonistic audience. For a more detailed treatment of Ramus' Cryptic, or Prudential, Method, see John Webster, "The Method of a Poete: An Inquiry into Tudor Conceptions of Poetic Order," *ELR* 11 (Winter, 1981): 22–43.

22. This phrase, "in the polish of the work of art they produce," is Temple's paraphrase of Sidney's "with the vigor of their own inuention" (156). Note that for Temple "inuention" is the poem itself—the thing made—and not, as most twentieth-century readers would understand the word, the capacity of mind, or imagination, which the poet uses to produce the poem. Note as well that "vigor," a term that for us connotes a kind of organic exuberence, is rendered by Temple as "polish" (*expolitio*). Clearly Temple seems to have understood Sidney's metaphor quite differently from the way we are now likely to take it. His understanding focuses on the poet's victory over other arts through his refined, craftsman-like making—an understanding consistent with Sidney's emphasis on the etymology of "poet" as "maker." What is certainly not in Temple is any suggestion that the poet's victory is achieved by a unique "imaginative" capacity of mind available to poetic temperaments alone. Though there is in Sidney a claim for poetic uniqueness, Temple's paraphrase makes clear that for him, at least, Sidney is claiming no privileged epistemological or ontological capacity of insight.

23. Temple's reference is to his lengthy argument with Sidney over the definition of poetry. See pp. 81–83.

24. By the phrase "fictional in every part" Temple means "with no connection at all to truth." The question raised here is of how one knows a poetic image is "true." As Temple will make clear later, he does not think this question can be answered as long as Sidney tries to keep poetry distinct from logic, since (he argues) the truth of something can only be established through logical analysis. See below, p. 137.

25. The two pages Temple devotes here to argument with Sidney's definition of poetry are central to his description of poetry's "logical" character. Throughout, Temple makes extensive use of the verb *fingere*, a verb difficult to render simply in English. It can mean "to feign," "to make," "to conceive," "to narrate," and the noun *fictio* which derives from it is similarly flexible. As *ars fictionis*, then, poetry is an "art of fiction," but it is also an "art of making," or, even, "of conceiving." Sidney does not use the phrase "art of fiction," but given his emphasis on the derivation of "poet" from *poiein*, "to make," the sense of *fingere* as "making" is probably what leads Temple to use *ars fictionis* as a paraphrase for Sidney's "art of imitation." See Introduction, part ii, for discussion of this and other issues in these pages.

26. Literally, to define poetry as a making "violates the Law of Justice." Such a definition, Temple argues, assigns to poetry what properly belongs to logic. See the Glossary entry for the Laws of Truth, Justice and Wisdom.

27. Literally, to say that teaching is an end of poetry "violates the Law of Justice," and to say that delighting is an end of poetry "violates the Law of Wisdom." For the first, as Temple explains in the next sentence, because teaching is an end of logic, it cannot also be an end of poetry, except insofar as poetry uses logic. Thus, this part of the definition fails to deal with what is essential to poetry—i.e., teaching is not unique to poetry alone. As for delight, Temple goes on to explain, because it is caused by many things besides poetry, it is too general to be thought of as a defining effect of poetry alone. Thus this part of Sidney's definition fails as well. See the Glossary entry for the Laws of Truth, Justice, and Wisdom.

28. Literally, to distribute poetry by subject violates the Law of Wisdom. Poetry does indeed have the subjects Sidney gives it, but so does logic. But because this distribution describes both poetry and logic, it applies more generally than to either art alone, and thus it is not properly a distribution of poetry at all. Again, see the Glossary entry for the Laws of Truth, Justice, and Wisdom.

29. Temple argues that Sidney violates the Law of Justice by mixing here the arts of theology and philosophy with the art of fictional making, since neither theology nor philosophy are "feigned."

30. By "an explanation of final causes from final causes" Temple means that Sidney explains the final causes, or purposes, of poetry—i.e., teaching and delighting—in terms of their own final causes. Thus the final cause of delight is "to moue men to take...goodnes in hande," and the final cause of teaching is "to make them know that goodnes whereunto they are mooued" (159).

31. Temple's objection in this passage is to the logical imprecision of Sidney's distribution of poets both by the subjects they treat and by the meter and style appropriate to each kind. (The logical classes established by such a double

distribution are not necessarily inconsistent but are very much likely to be. You can create a simple distribution of fruit, for example, by color — grapefruit and bananas are both yellow — or by shape — grapefruit and oranges are round. But you cannot have a similarly simple distribution by both color and shape, since some members of one class may have characteristics which exclude them from the other — bananas are not round; oranges are not yellow.)

32. Literally, such a distribution would violate the Law of Wisdom. Temple's objection here is that if poets can be distributed by subject, so can logicians; but if logicians are so distributed, then differences between subjects have already been accounted for through different kinds of logician, and to repeat the distribution in the case of poets will be redundant. Sidney thus violates the Law of Wisdom because his distribution of subjects operates at a more general level than is appropriate to poetry alone. Each of these subjects — serious matters, comic matters, and so on — can be handled in true narration as well as in poetic narration, and in prose as well as in verse, and thus to group them all under poetry is to be overly restrictive and, therefore, misleading.

33. Having rejected any distribution by subject, Temple endorses Sidney's distribution of poetry by meter. Temple does not give his own definition for poetry, but here and later he implies that he would define it as anything written in verse (see note 35).

34. Temple's Latin here is *oratio*, the only time he uses the word as a description of Sidney's treatise. I translate it as "discourse" instead of the more literal "oration" because Temple's use of the term elsewhere in the *Analysis* rarely carries anything like the modern, historically more narrow meaning of the word as a rhetorically structured speech in 4, 5, or 7 parts. Temple's usual term for Sidney's work is *tractatio*. Given the modern inclination to view Sidney's work as a 7-part judicial oration, Temple's rather different perception is worth note. For more discussion of this issue see John Webster, "Oration and Method in Sidney's *Apology*: A Contemporary's Account," *MP* 79 (1981): 1-15.

35. In pp. 81-83, Temple has argued that fictive makings are the product of logical invention and that they are not something over which poetry alone has dominion. Moreover, he has also pointed out that poetry can be true as well as feigned. But (he reasons) if making is thus not essential to poetry, and if teaching and delighting are similarly inessential to poetry, then meter is the only characteristic Sidney is left with to define poetry and poetry alone.

36. Poets (Temple objects) can be said to excel others in the value (*dignitas*) of their matter only if fictional subjects really do (as Sidney says) excel true subjects in value. Temple questions whether this is in fact the case.

37. Sidney defines Architectonic as "the highest end of the mistres Knowledge...which stands...in the knowledge of a mans selfe, in the Ethicke and politick consideration, with the end of well dooing and not of well knowing onely" (161). Thus because all arts have "a priuate end in themselues," "they are all subordinate to the highest end [of the Architectonic]."

38. Temple's Latin literally implies that the philosopher is arguing with the historian. Sidney's text gives us philosophers arguing among themselves. Temple is so careful elsewhere, and *alter* is sufficiently inspecific anyway, that it is more likely he has miswritten here than misread.

39. Temple's comparison to law refers to Sidney's argument cited above

on p. 99 that the lawyer "dooth not endeuor to make men good." Temple's point is that whatever ordinary treatments of either ethics or law do, good treatments should provide examples as well as precepts, and in judging either art Sidney should consider not the currently available treatments, but what should be available if such a treatment is to cover what its subject truly entails. Sidney is wrong, therefore, to criticize either ethics or law for failing to provide examples. Throughout this reply, it is important to recognize that Temple does not argue for the superiority of either ethics or law to poetry. He wants only to argue against Sidney's claims for poetry's uniqueness.

40. The objection here concerns Sidney's claim that Poetry "dealeth with *katholou*, that is to say, the vniuersall consideration" (167). If dealing with something through universals produces obscurity in ethics, Temple argues, then it should produce obscurity in poetry as well.

41. That is, no general rule can be induced from a single event.

42. Temple is making two points about his earlier remarks. First, in response to Sidney's definition of poetry, Temple had argued that when poets teach, they do so as logicians; therefore, he now reminds Sidney, though poets may teach virtue both through precept and example, they do so not because they are poets, but because they are using logic. Second, he has argued that a proper treatment of ethics is "perfect" (in the old sense of "complete") because it gives examples as well as precepts, and thus, Temple now notes again, the poet's similar ability to couple the general with the particular does not make him better than the moral philosopher.

43. See above, p. 99.

44. In this section Temple uses the Latin *imitatio* to describe the relation between a poem and its reader, and not the relation between the poem and its informing Idea. One wonders whether the English word "imitation" had the same ambiguity of reference. Given that Sidney's argument for poetry turns heavily on its ability to move men to a moral imitation of what poetry figures forth, it is possible that some of this sense of the reader/text relation is implicit in Sidney's earlier definition of poetry as an "art of imitation." In such a case, Sidney would be defining poetry not only as an "art that imitates," but also as an "art that inspires imitation."

45. Sidney's argument that feigned examples teach as well as true ones is parallel to the assertion Ramist logics also make when discussing comparisons. See the example from Fraunce cited in part I of the Introduction. Again, what Sidney sees as a poetic resource, Temple would see as a logical resource.

46. See p. 125.

47. Again, Temple's argument is that fictional making is the concern of logic, not poetry. No art can make fictions except by using the rules of logical invention.

48. Temple's argument in reply to Sidney's position that "moouing is of a higher degree then teaching" is again a defense of logic and philosophy against claims for poetry's superiority. The issues here are discussed in the Introduction, part II.

49. Sidney uses the story of Menenius Agrippa to illustrate the power of poetry; Abraham Fraunce uses the same story to illustrate the logical power of feigned comparisons (*LL* 73a; cited in the Introduction, part I).

50. Beginning here, Temple lists five calumnies, numbering each one. Sidney

also numbers these calumnies, but includes this particular complaint about rhyme and meter as part of his preface dealing with the Fault-finders and Fools who scorn poetry, and he begins his own numbering with what Temple takes to be the second calumny. Though Temple and Sidney number the arguments differently, the arguments themselves are the same, and in the same order.

51. "Helping causes": that is, a cause which only contributes to an effect, but (in this case) is not itself necessary to that effect. Thus verse helps, but is not necessary to, memory.

52. Temple believes that Sidney's definition of lying is too narrow and therefore violates the Law of Wisdom. As Temple's discussion makes clear, he would define lying not as the affirmation of something false, as Sidney does, but as the uttering of any axiom which does not truly reflect the nature of what it presumes to describe. See Introduction, part II, for discussion.

53. "Feigned comparison from the lesser": Sidney's comparison is between the amount of contempt for poetry in England and the (lesser) amount of contempt elsewhere. The comparison is "feigned," of course, because the earth is only imagined to weep.

54. In explaining that the final cause of Sidney's "attentiue translation" is to imitate not the phrasing or rhetorical devices but the judgment and prudence of these authors, Temple aligns Sidney's theory of stylistic imitation with Gabriel Harvey's in the *Ciceronianus* (See Introduction Note 2 for reference). There Harvey places himself in the company of Erasmus, Freigius, and Ramus, and in opposition to the Italian Ciceronians and those Harvey takes to be their English followers. Again, this is an argument which bears interestingly on the question of how "imitation" was understood by Sidney and those closest to him, for it differentiates two distinct kinds of imitation, the first an imitation of surface features, such as subject and stylistic devices, the second an imitation of the "essence" of an author, or as Harvey puts it, of an author's "causes" rather than of his "effects."

55. This qualifying remark and quotation from Virgil are Temple's, not Sidney's.

56. Ramist rhetorics dealt only with ornaments that could "deck" a speech; because Ramists (like other Humanist logicians) felt that similes could explain or make clear—do more, that is, than simply ornament speech—they treated similes as logical arguments, and not as rhetorical devices.

57. Temple's use in this paragraph of the terms "invention," "judgment," "axiom," "syllogism," and "method" are all technical references to his logical system. For definitions see the Glossary; for an explanation of the relation of these terms to each other see Introduction, part I.

58. One cannot, Temple explains, have a "treatise" unless there exists a subject for the treatise to be about. One can, however, have a subject without the existence of any treatise about that subject. Thus a subject is logically prior to any treatise on that subject. Because the principle of Method says that the clearest way to explain anything is to begin with what is logically prior and most general, and only then proceed by degrees to more specific matters, Sidney (Temple explains) proceeds here in accord with Method by first announcing his subject, and only then proceeding with the treatise proper. This question of what is logically prior is recurrent in these last pages.

59. Temple's argument that Sidney should discuss the issue of verse before

he distributes poetry is important to his implicit claim that poetry is best defined as versified discourse, and not as an art of fictional making (see above, notes 33 and 35). For Sidney is not in fact being very rigorous. He says that verse is not essential to poetry, but by saying this only after he has already dealt with theological and philosophical poetry, Sidney seems to evade an admission that theological poetry and philosophical poetry are poetic *only* because they are in verse. In these two cases, since neither is "feigned," and since Sidney offers no other defining characteristic, verse would indeed seem the essential and single "poetic" feature. But (Temple would ask) if verse is the essential characteristic of poetry in theological and philosophical poetry, then why is it not also the essential characteristic in the third part of poetry as well?

60. Temple's last pages mildly reorganize Sidney's treatise. He puts the definition of poetry before its adjuncts, and he places philosophical poetry before divine poetry — changes he has explained in the section immediately preceding this one. Otherwise his major change is a redirection of Sidney's emphasis. Where Sidney spends many pages comparing the Poet with the Philosopher, the Historian, and the Lawyer, Temple overlooks these topics in his outline and concentrates instead on poetry's parts — something Sidney himself does only *pro forma*. For more discussion of the implications of this reorganization, again see my "Oration and Method in Sidney's *Apology*."

61. Temple has inadvertently reversed Sidney's comparison. The Poet concerned to feign things should be to other poets no less unlike than is the excellent painter to the average painter.

62. Temple's phrasing here clearly implies that he intends his *Analysis* to be a constructive and practical criticism, and that he believes Sidney may well make use of it to rework his text. Since the quotations in the *Analysis* taken from Sidney's manuscript show no substantial variation from what became the published version, it seems fairly certain that Sidney did not rewrite anything. At the same time, since it is difficult to imagine Temple's undertaking such a project without Sidney's knowledge, the very existence of Temple's work implies that Sidney was open to thoughts of revision, and may even have requested Temple's suggestions.

mRts

meðieval & Renaissance texts & stuðies
is the publishing program of the
Center for Medieval & Early Renaissance Studies
at the State University of New York at Binghamton.

mRts emphasizes books that are needed —
texts, translations, and major research tools.

mRts aims to publish the highest quality scholarship
in attractive and durable format at modest cost.

The **Analysis** presents for the first time the text and English translation of William Temple's *Analysis tractationis de Poesi contextae a nobilissimo viro Philippe Sidneio equite aurato*, the earliest commentary on Sidney's *Apology for Poetry*. Written between 1584 and 1586, while Temple was Sidney's secretary, the work treats the whole of Sidney's text, sometimes objecting, sometimes paraphrasing, always attempting to describe the course of the argument. Temple's **Analysis** makes an important claim on modern readers, not only because of the centrality of Sidney's work or the scope of Temple's remarks on theoretical positions in the *Apology*, but also because it is an outstanding instance of Tudor practical criticism, of which we have too few examples. Temple's book demonstrates both the likely strengths and weaknesses of such efforts. Throughout, we see how similes were parsed, what purposes parts of a discourse were understood to serve, how rhetorical terms with special implications were used. Hence the **Analysis** will interest scholars in Renaissance literature, rhetoric, literary theory, and history. Professor Webster's book also provides a substantial introduction, which shows how Temple's analytic system relates to the logic and rhetoric of the period, and which explains and evaluates Temple's discussion of Sidney's theoretical positions. Beyond these and information on Temple's life and the text, the introduction also supplies a full glossary of Temple's terminology.

John Webster is Associate Professor of English at the University of Washington. He has published articles on Elizabethan literature in *Studies in English Literature*, *English Literary Renaissance*, and *Modern Philology*, and is preparing a book on poetry and logic in Tudor England.

DATE DUE